RIGHT IN THE HEAD

Sebastian Groes is a teacher and scholar of contemporary culture. He is Professor of English Literature at the University of Wolverhampton, where he is Director of the Centre for Transnational and Transcultural Research. He leads several research projects including the Arts and Humanities Research Council funded *Novel Perceptions*, which investigates unconscious biases in British readers. He has written more than ten academic books, including *The Making of London*, *British Fictions of the Sixties* and works on writers including Ian McEwan and Kazuo Ishiguro. He has published short stories and non-fiction in English and Dutch, is currently working on a novel. He is also co-editor of *Writing Under Fire: Poetry and Prose from Ukraine and the Black Country*. *Right in the Head* is his first work of non-fiction. As part of this project, Bas is developing an online creative writing tool for people with brain trauma.

RIGHT IN THE HEAD

My Stroke Journey

Sebastian Groes

London
*Jet*stone
2023

A *Jet*stone paperback original.

ISBN 9781910858257

The right of Sebastian Groes to be identified as author
in this work has been asserted in accordance with the
Copyright, Designs and Patents Act, 1988.

Cover photos of the author © Tessa Posthuma de Boer.

Contents

Part I *À votre santé*

Chapter One	*Portomonee*	11
Chapter Two	Portraits of My Brain Just After the Attack	19
Chapter Three	The **PHILIPS** Phenomenon	36
Chapter Four	How Are You Getting Back?	45

Part II The Art of Getting Lost

Chapter Five	Cosmic Irony	55
Chapter Six	A Trickster in My Head	67
Chapter Seven	The Brain, Within Its Groove	78
Chapter Eight	Maps of the Mind	90
Chapter Nine	A Concise History of Stroke	101
Chapter Ten	Emotional Dyscontrol	113
Chapter Eleven	*Shits* and *Goddamnits*	125
Chapter Twelve	Writing Without Strange Blunders	136

Part III An Odyssey of Maybes

Chapter Thirteen	And I Shall Need All My Brains to Get Through	153
Chapter Fourteen	A Wound without Pain	164
Chapter Fifteen	Prolonged Bleeding, Easy Bruising	175
Chapter Sixteen	Information Overload	186
Chapter Seventeen	Sing for Life	194

Epilogue   201
Acknowledgements   205
List of Figures   207
Further Reading   208

For José

One man scorned and covered with scars still strove with his last ounce of courage to reach the unreachable stars; and the world was better for this.

Miguel de Cervantes, *Don Quixote* (1605)

Part I
À votre santé

Chapter One
Portomonee

Dit is belachelijk. This is preposterous. I catch myself standing in the shower of a converted farmhouse in the south of France. I'm on holiday at a friend's place, relaxing after a crushing time at work. Lukewarm water is trickling down the runnel of my spine, the drops making tracks across my skin that tickle. I observe this sensation – this tickle, which is odd yet oddly pleasant; normally such everyday habitual activities pass by unnoticed. But now I'm conscious that I'm just standing there, doing nothing, wasting water, feeling leaden, sluggish – dead weight in my skull. Not fully woken up. Monstrous headache. I look outside the rickety window and see the weather is mimicking my state of mind: the Mediterranean sky that ought to be the lightest blue is densely packed with low-hanging, dove-grey clouds. The sun is not even attempting to disperse the murk.

Through the low doorway, built for diminutive seventeenth-century farmers, my wife José appears. The status of our relationship is currently uncertain: after a gruelling eight-year infertility tragedy, we fell apart. She's living in Amsterdam, I stayed in London. But we're here, making an attempt to see if we can get back together again. Car keys in hand, she's about to drive to the village bakery to buy *un pain aux céréales, une baguette et deux pains au chocolat.* She looks at my naked body, the body she knows so intimately, water running down its skin.

'Do we need anything else?' she asks.

I can feel my nakedness like I'm being unpeeled. I want to say that there's change in my wallet. But something is wrong with my voice. In my head I can formulate the sentence perfectly, but no sounds will cross my lips. I try to utter *portomonee* – the French-derived Dutch word for 'wallet', but from my mouth nothing more emerges than *p - p - p*. Through the doorway I can see my *portomonee* lying on the kitchen table containing bank cards, ID, National Insurance card, my driver's licence – evidence of my full identity. The wallet also contains a tiny red envelope with an equally tiny card saying 'Love You Always' that José gave to me when I was awarded my Ph.D. in 2006. We bought this particular *portomonee* together on our honeymoon, in Florence, eleven years ago. But the four-syllable word that should name this object is proving too much.

I can just about say *Ik* ('I') and very slowly pronounce the word *heb* ('have') but I cannot complete even the simplest of sentences. The words sound unfamiliar, as if spoken by someone else's mouth in a voice that isn't quite mine either. I panic when I realise I'm suffering from some kind of curious locked-in syndrome and that, more worryingly, I've turned into a mute. It's a troubled dream.

Inside my head I scream: 'What the hell is going on?'

In José's eyes I spy fear and in her tensed-up body I read distress. 'What is going on, Bas?' she asks. 'Can you act normal, please? What's wrong with you?'

Frustration turns to anger. I want to tell her that there is change in my stupid wallet which is on the stupid kitchen table but nothing sensible emerges from my mouth. Something's definitely wrong with my senses. It feels as if I'm travelling down a highway at great speed at night but with one headlight broken: I can see but the view is dimmed.

I try to point but even my gestures are failing. José follows the direction of what my finger seems to want to point at, sees the *portomonee*. She grabs the wallet and flees the scene, off to the bakery. I hope that if we both pretend this is simple, a minor incident, the result of an epic hangover, we will be able to continue with life as normal. But I know something's not right inside my head even though I'm making a strenuous effort to deny this thought.

This morning everything feels heavier, as if God has turned up gravitational forces to eleven. But even *Spinal Tap* cannot bring a smile to my face. My movement is slower; I'm walking around the house listlessly.

Luckily, reading is still no problem. I sit in the living room on a rickety sofa underneath the skylight. I'm reading Haruki Murakami's *Norwegian Wood*, a coming-of-age novel. My eyes are scanning the lines of black ink and have no trouble turning the signs into a credible reality: a story that feels unbroken and authentic. I am fully wrapped up in the comfort of reading, in which my mind and the book are extensions of each other – a fusing of whatever electrochemical processes are happening within my skull and the imaginary architecture conjured up by the thousands of graphemes on the pages in front of me. Reading feels comfortable, and it tricks me into thinking nothing's wrong with me. This is something at least: reading is central to my life, as a Professor of Literature and as a human being. I read for work and I read to live. Fiction is my window onto the world: I use books to understand life and people, to judge events, make decisions. Novels are my guide: I navigate my life by listening to the voices and thoughts of the writers and characters that inhabit these imagined worlds.

But whenever I look up from the page I realize that something isn't right. When I return to the world outside *Norwegian Wood*'s fictional reality, my world continues to stutter and falter. My reality is unravelling. My head still hurts but it isn't necessarily the pain inside I'm worried about: the world around me feels different. Just a tad. Like the dial on the radio has accidentally been shifted by a fraction from its usual station: noise creeps in, interference for the 24-hour news broadcast that is the voice inside my head. I'm not sure if fiction is able to make sense of what's happening to me.

Later that morning I check my emails. A query by a

colleague working on our memory research project has come in. I write back:

> Hello Peter,
> I trust all's wel.
> Thakn you for you're feedback. It seems taht with reasonably little work yuo hsoudl be albi a end give dat

I stop writing. That's not quite what I thought I'd typed; certainly not the sentences that I saw in my head whilst happily tapping away at the keyboard. Only now, looking back over the text, do I realize that I am making a plethora of grammatical and spelling mistakes – utter gibberish. Like a bloody baby. My writing is derailing as well.

I ask José to look at the mangled missive. 'Jesus, what the...' she replies. 'Best to take it easy. Shall we go for a walk?'

It's a lovely idea, but I feel the urgent need to stay indoors. I save the email and close the laptop. On my skin I see goose bumps, signs of the panic I'm trying to suppress. I am a scholar of English Literature, make my living by teaching, doing research and writing books. I feel sick. This could be the end of a twenty-five-year-long devotion to literature. Nausea panics in my gut.

For an hour or so I walk around the house absent-mindedly, trying to put my finger on what is happening. Briefly I return to Murakami, and find temporary solace in reading, but I notice I'm restless. José is pottering about in the background, and reading, but she too puts her novel down after ten minutes. It seems she is instinctively leaving me to myself, seeing how self-absorbed and worried I am. She feels excluded – and she is, indeed.

At midday, I ask José to walk with me down the narrow road that connects the four houses belonging to this tiniest of hamlets, *Le cabanié*. The sun shines, just a few clouds in the air, a pleasant breeze to slice through the tranquillity. It's so quiet, no people for miles. I've been coming to *Le cabanié* for three years straight, I know this place well, my senses are attuned to the light, the sounds of a resident dormouse and owls, and the rasping sounds of crickets ebbing and flowing in the air. I know very well the way the wind follows a particular route through the valley, slowly pushing up the clouds.

But the world is out of kilter. I don't know what's wrong. *Alsof... alsof...* As if. As if. I don't know what I want to say. The explanation escapes me. It's beyond the reach of words.

The way my feet touch the asphalt is not quite right: *alsof...* as if the ground beneath my feet is half an inch too far below me. I'm not afraid of heights but I feel queasy.

It hits me: *Het licht... is niet... in orde.* The light... is not... right. The sky's blueness is off. It's as if I can see the light – a solid whiteness: particles hitting the trees' leaves, the bricks of the house and the skin of José's face. She stands in front of me, and looks me in the eye, as if she can tell what's wrong with me by looking into my brain. But she doesn't know what to do with the situation either: the only thing she can do is observe me closely. What strikes me, though, is that this exceptional situation brings with it a stronger sensory awareness – and this also entails a heightened attentiveness, and self-consciousness. The world is out of joint, but not on a Shakespearean scale: only ever so slightly, as if some fiend is toying with my senses. I do not feel like 'myself'.

Time passes. We nap. The headache subsides a bit. I feel a little better. Though still preoccupied with the curious turn of events this morning, I remember that I was supposed to send a friend money for a concert ticket. I raise the bank transfer and write to him:

> i've put the money into your acconut i thing it should be into there stay away. thank you for much.

Not much better, after all.

In the evening, we sit outside on the terrace, watching the sunset, and eat a simple dinner. We listen to some *chansons* by Charles Aznavour and José's favourite *chansonnier* Jacques Brel. They take our minds of the weird atmosphere for a bit but I'm preoccupied, still. We Google my symptoms, and various websites point in the direction of a TIA, a transient ischaemic attack (a mini-stroke), but that's impossible as I'm too young. I'm thirty-nine, and will celebrate my fortieth birthday in two months' time by playing a reunion gig with my skate punk band. But I promise we'll go to a hospital the next day if this weirdness persists.

At nine, exhaustion knocks me out, and I sink into the blackest sleep, without any dreams whatsoever.

The next day the skewed perception is still present – an ineffable weirdness I can only lasso with metaphors. My speech is slightly better but still slow, slurred. I'm making mistakes, mixing up phrases, using incorrect words. The dull feeling inside my skull has subsided a bit but I know something's not right.

We decide to drive to the hospital. Into my backpack I stuff a few T-shirts, underwear and socks, as well as *Norwegian Wood*. With José seated next to me, I drive out of the valley – an act that in hindsight seems ridiculously hubristic and plain stupid – but I want to master the situation. And soon I understand that even in the driver's seat I no longer feel in control. My friend's house lies five kilometres down a road that winds itself, gorgeously, as only French roads do, into a *vallée*. I've driven this way dozens of times, and I know every bend by heart.

But now the road that I know so well is no longer the same old road. I feel the steering wheel in my hands, and I notice the way in which my feet are clumsily touching the pedals. I have trouble navigating the bends – as if I no longer properly feel the tyres' traction. My clammy palms clasp the wheel too tightly. The connection between me and this machine, just like the relationship between me and my body, is disrupted. José should be driving.

Looking back, even after many years, I remember that trip to hospital extremely clearly: the overwhelming feeling of impatience and agitation fuming. I won't deny that I'm an assertive road user, but during the journey everyone seemed to drive so leisurely – not a care in the world.

At the hospital, I can't find a parking space, and I become even more frustrated. Once I find a spot, I push past flocks of pilgrims looking for Albi's cathedral and elderly tourists in search of their cultural fix. The answer to my condition is only two hundred metres away. 'Move out of the way!' I shout silently. I am so aggravated by this situation. I'd never been to hospital, except to get my tonsils removed when I was six. I shouldn't even be near a hospital! *Dit is belachelijk.*

At the hospital a young doctor with lively, probing eyes takes me into an examination room. I try to explain what has happened but I'm actually not sure what has occurred and even if I were, I couldn't verbalise it properly in French. So, I point to the left side of my head.

She makes me do eight different tasks. First, I have to walk in a straight line, like they make drunk drivers do in America. This isn't a problem, though uncertainty creeps in: this simple exercise is questioning the continuum between my mind and body. The very artifice of this performance – to walk in an imaginary line – is messing with my inner compass.

During the next assignment, I have to follow her finger with my eyes, from left to right, up, down, do the same with one eye closed, then the other. She's satisfied with that too. She asks me to close my left eye and touch the tip of my nose with my right index finger, and vice-versa. I push her hand upward, then downward, to check my motor skills and muscle strength. All fine.

But there is a final test. I have to put the right index finger of my right hand next to my right ear just beyond my peripheral vision where I cannot see it. She asks me to move my left index finger towards it in order to let the fingertips meet. Confidently I move my index finger towards its counterpart, but they miss each other by a mile. A worried frown imprints itself on the doctor's face, and she makes a note with her *stylo*. I mirror the exercise, failing again. The young doctor says nothing but walks towards a wall-mounted phone and rings someone.

A few minutes later, a tall, lean Frenchman sporting a sophisticated-looking pair of glasses on the tip of his nose walks into the room. This neurologist, who could double as a modernist architect, discusses the results of my tests with the other doctor. I find their whispering overly conspiratorial.

I haven't seen any panic buttons but someone has definitely pressed one. Reality is on fast-forward. I'm ordered to lie on a gurney, whilst two nurses strap me to a heart monitor and carry me away down the corridor, leaving my wife standing in the corridor, silent and helpless. Watching the strip lighting on the ceiling whizz by, helplessly, I panic. Am I dying?

A few minutes later I'm in a large room, home to an imposing machine making grumpy noises. A radiologist, sheltered in his booth behind double glazing, sends orders through an intercom and the nurses make me lie on a slab. The machine gobbles me up and does its business, uncaring and unfeeling. Locked inside this machine I imagine I can feel X-rays pushing through the gelatinous matter inside my skull, probing, latching onto the billions of brain cells.

Twenty minutes later the CT scan is ready, and we are looking at a black-and-white photograph of a slice of my brain that the doctor holds against the light. His index finger traces lines on this curious image, as if he is the cartographer of a strange, undiscovered country. He is pointing at two dark black areas, on the right and left side of the image. My neurological sherpa cannot believe his findings and states with barely disguised excitement: 'Dr Groes, you have suffered two strokes.'

Chapter Two
Portraits of My Brain Just After the Attack

My stroke had come out of the blue. There were no symptoms that announced what was to happen – no headache, no glitches in my speech. I also knew almost nothing about what a stroke was. I seemed vaguely to remember it was something to do with old people with one half of their face sagging like a deflating balloon. I associated it with limps and slurred speech. When I thought of the Dutch word for a stroke – *beroerte* – I felt an uncanny feeling of disgust: the word is associated with feeling 'sick to death'.

My neurologist did not tell me the basics of what a stroke exactly was. I think he assumed I knew, which I didn't, so I started to search the internet for information. I understood that a stroke happens when parts of the brain are starved of oxygen and atrophy, that is to say, start to wither and die. It can either be poor or restricted flow of blood or a complete blockage. This lack of oxygen can occur in two ways. In about 80 percent of stroke cases, a small blood clot gets stuck in a blood vessel in the brain. This type of accident is called an 'ischaemic' stroke – we can call them the 'clotters'. But we also have the 'bleeders', which are cases in which a blood vessel in the brain bursts, thereby cutting of the blood supply. The idea sounded like pure horror, the brain drowning in its own blood. This version is called a 'haemorrhagic' stroke and happens in one fifth of stroke cases. I also read about a condition called 'subarachnoid haemorrhage', which is most commonly caused by a brain aneurysm whereby an artery in the brain ruptures and causes bleeding into the space between the brain and the skull. The American actress Sharon Stone has one of these. If the symptoms last for only a couple of hours – people feel dizzy or start to utter gibberish for a while – this is a TIA, a transient ischaemic attack, a mini-stroke that passes by quickly.

I read that the main cause of stroke was high blood pressure. Smoking tobacco, obesity or high cholesterol didn't help. A family history of heart or blood disease puts you at increased risk of stroke. The symptoms were also identified: a loss of feeling on one side of the body, problems with understanding or speaking, or sight loss to one side of one's field of vision. I guessed it had something to do with the two halves of the brain: only one part would be under attack, and the effects would manifest themselves on the other side of the body – this was how the brain and body worked.

I absorbed a lot of facts: about how many people suffered a stroke each year; about the survival rate; about the difference between stroke in the richer and low-income countries. About 6.9 million people had an ischaemic stroke (I was one of them), and 3.4 million suffered an haemorrhagic version, yet both types killed about 3 million people a year (the haemorrhagic is much more dangerous). I understood that two thirds of strokes happened in older people (over 65s), but also read that strokes were occurring increasingly to younger people like me – I was part of a trend. An article in *The Lancet* said that half of people who've had a stroke live less than a year. It put the living fear into me.

I was in need of someone who could help me explain what had happened to me – and what was happening – and put my mind at ease. Because even though I couldn't predict this right now, over the next few months many ideas I had about myself would collapse and I'd be confronted with self-doubt as well as questions about the nature of human experience. I would come to understand that the persona I had carefully built over the years was a construction. The protagonist of my own story was a lot less stable than I had come to believe. And all of this because of a minuscule blood clot. A tiny dirty bullet.

My training in understanding storytelling would perhaps be of help, I thought. English Literature professors have lots to say about how literature can capture subjective experience, but I also wondered if any of my knowledge could help me understand my new condition. Could the literature that had guided me thus far now help me make sense of my differently working brain, or was nothing I'd read relevant anymore? I needed to understand what had happened to my brain but also how my stroke might impact on my personal and professional life.

Lying in my hospital bed after the neurologist's diagnosis, I was thinking of James Joyce, a writer who'd been an important guide for me. The nurses had wheeled me to the Stroke Unit on the fourth floor and put me on a bed strapped to a heart monitor in a private room. They injected me with some kind of fluid and took my blood pressure, which turned out to be too high. José hovered around the room, unsure of what to do, like me. After she left I lay on my hospital bed, alone and confused. I was doubly speechless: I didn't know what to think about the situation I found myself in and, even if I had wanted to, I couldn't speak properly. The diagnosis felt like a death sentence. I had reached my use-by date.

A strange feeling came over me when I realised I felt dead, but still curiously alive at the same time when I considered a potential journey of discovery. Joyce's *A Portrait of the Artist as a Young Man* was on my mind. The novel tells the story of a journey in which Joyce's adolescent *alter ego* Stephen Dedalus tries various routes not so much to 'find' himself but to make himself. His doubts about his training as a Jesuit priest make him realise that he needs to take an aesthetic route: the way of the arts and culture is his life-path.

During the 'bird-girl' episode he looks at a young woman on a beach and discovers his artistic vision, which he is unable to express in words. Dedalus thinks: 'Her image had passed into his soul for ever and no word had broken the holy silence of his ecstasy. Her eyes had called him and his soul had leaped at the call. To live, to err, to fall, to triumph, to recreate life out of life!' The truth he sees lies beyond reality and before words; it's an aesthetic. Dedalus glimpses his vision but the moment expresses something even more beautifully troubling because it refuses to provide a full, easy explanation for the knowledge brought by his epiphany. The moment of transformation raises the possibility that the associated forms of understanding cannot not be represented through words – an uneasy, challenging task for an artist whose medium is language.

After this moment of discovery, Dedalus decides to leave his homeland of Ireland and live abroad in self-imposed exile, as Joyce did himself. The writer became a nomad, living in Trieste and Paris, where he wrenched himself away from the realistic style of nineteenth-century writing and focused on his subjective experience.

I read *A Portrait* when studying English Literature in Amsterdam. The novel rubbed off on me. After I graduated, I failed to finish the short stories and screenplays I was working on, mostly out of fear of failure. I didn't get a decent job, and my ambitions to make it with my band ground to a halt when the record company that had signed us shelved our prospective first album . I felt frustrated. I was hitting glass as well as concrete ceilings everywhere. With Joyce in the back of my mind I decided to emigrate to the UK, the country where my artistic and intellectual ambitions could perhaps be taken to a new level.

Moving abroad turned out to be the best decision José and I could have chosen. We made new friends in Norwich, at the University of East Anglia, where we did our degrees, and landed intellectually satisfying jobs. José worked for various government departments, the Independent Police Complaints Commission, and finally as an Assistant to a London Assembly Member, looking out over the Thames and London Bridge from City Hall. (Heroic fact: when Boris Johnson became Mayor of London in 2008, she refused to shake his hand – she said that she doesn't 'shake hands with the enemy'. Yes, she is *that* cool.) In Liverpool, I became a Lecturer, then a Senior Lecturer, and moved to London – my Ph.D. was on the capital city in literature – to become Associate Professor at a London university. We had made it.

But now, with my brain smashed, I was back to where I was ten years ago. Had all my hard work been for nothing? What use was my knowledge of literature to me if I couldn't speak or write?

Lying on my hospital bed, I reflected on the life I was leading in the run-up to the stroke. It was, to understate things somewhat, a bit bonkers. My ambitions were making many Shakespeare characters from Edmund to Lady Macbeth look like lazy, bungling loafers. Over the past years I had been in an extreme rush: I had published nearly four books in the previous two years (one critic started his review with 'Here's another book by Sebastian Groes...'), organised several conferences, and been through a marital crisis. I had been living two lives, one in London and one in Amsterdam, where I'd just had a sabbatical. I was involved in lots of travel, organising events across the UK; I'd been shortlisted for a Professorship (I didn't get it); I had a slipped disc and was on severe painkillers whilst on the side editing a volume of a Flemish literary magazine on the cultural history of the Rhine, just for fun.

I felt most happy travelling, being on the road, being in between places. The feeling of lightness that came with not being locked into one place was a drug I was hopelessly addicted to.

Now, I wondered if my nomadic lifestyle has caught up with me. Maybe my brain was trying to tell me something, that I needed to settle down, take it easy, and give myself a break. I hadn't listened and now my brain had given me a break on behalf of itself.

Suddenly, lying on that hospital bed and barely able to speak, I was no longer sure anymore. I understood that my recent lifestyle might have overloaded my skull. I'd demanded too much of this organ that had now brutally imposed a time-out on my life. Perhaps I should have protected myself much sooner against grotesque quantities of excitation. Had I unconsciously wanted to bring this upon myself? My overly fanatical attitude to my work had come to take revenge, and I was confronted personally with what to me now seemed the very important role of the brain in life. Unwillingly I had become a neuromaniac, the term used scathingly by humanities scholars for neuroscientists who believed that the brain and the brain alone is the most important factor when it comes to understanding humans.

Again I wondered what the cause of the stroke was. Maybe it was thrombosis from sitting in my car on the fourteen-hour drive down to the south of France; I was driving for much too long, not stopping except to fill up with petrol. The endless sitting could have caused my blood to clot in the veins of my legs, leading to an embolic stroke – so-called 'deep vein thrombosis' (DVT), as I read on the internet. When I arrived at my holiday home I was exhausted, my legs were wobbly and I was dizzy. Maybe my heart had misfired or decided to enjoy a power nap. Maybe the mounting work stress had finally punished me, or the opposite: perhaps too much relaxation in France confused my blood circulation, which went on holiday as well. Who knew? Doctors, presumably – neurologists. Shadows on the hospital wall grew longer and the world darker until the room was black except for the lights of the machines that I was plugged into.

After the blackest sleep, I wake up at 6 am, surrounded by four white walls. It is unusually early. Fresh sunlight radiates on the walls. All is quiet. For a moment, everything is alright: my mind is still in between non-consciousness and full awareness so isn't registering what has happened. But then, with awareness emerging, the feeling of doom returns and I remember: I have suffered a stroke.

'Bonjour!' A smiling nurse walks in and silently looks over my night stats: blood pressure, heart rate, temperature, etc. It's been difficult to sleep strapped to the blood pressure monitor that automatically crushes my arm every hour.

In the early morning my energy levels are not too bad so I read on a bit in *Norwegian Wood*. The novel tells the story of a successful, thirty-seven-year-old Japanese man, Toru Watanabe, who looks back upon his troubled adolescence and the choices that brought him where he is today. The youthful Watanabe is seeking the right way to live. His choice is symbolised by two different paths offered by two girls: his unstable, quirky girlfriend Naoko, who promises transcendence from his mundane existence, and the more conventional, stable Midori, offering a 'sensible' path. Although the choice is made for him by an event outside his control, Watanabe remains torn between the two options these girls symbolise. Usually Murakami's stories explore alienation and the strange appeal of surrealist underworlds, suggesting that beneath the comfortable surface of everyday life dark worlds hide. This novel is different, though: *Norwegian Wood*'s story is set in reality, dark for sure but without a sense of hidden worlds. Though it has a lingering spectre of sadness, hurt and confusion below the surface, the novel's realism is smooth and hard as concrete.

The novel has more relevance for me the more I realise the potential implications of my stroke. I'm also reflecting on my life and the choices I have made. What stuff was under my control and what forces have shaped where I am today: my wife, my friends, my teachers. My present and past too seem to be engaged in some kind of warfare, whilst the reality of my life has also been torn down. Everything feels a bit surreal: the hospital setting that feels like a theatre, the nurses and doctors who are playing their roles, and me as submissive patient. The Dutch have a saying for this: it feels like 'I'm in the wrong movie' – an actor finding himself play a part in a completely different script.

At 7 a.m. two nurses collect me, one sprightly young guy and a chubby balding bloke, his breath heavy with Gauloises *brunes*. They take me to the MRI scanner. The pair shoot quips in French at each another. I don't understand them, but I know black irony when I hear it – and these comedians have been fine-tuning their routine for a long time, like childhood friends. They remind me of the two characters from *Hamlet*, the court jesters Rosencrantz and Guildenstern.

They cart me to the basement, next to the morgue and the incinerator that pumps hospital waste into the blue Mediterranean sky. Jolly. I can hear the MRI scanner making its industrial drone from afar – a low, rhythmic, driving sound. When the courtiers wheel me into the scanning room, a terrible sense of irony dawns on me again.

Earlier that year, I'd been involved in an experiment with one of these machines at University College London's Neuroscience department, where a colleague and I conducted an experiment into the writer Will Self's spatial awareness and navigational skills. Self is a psychogeographer, which means that he compulsively walks cities to understand how the city's structure and architecture impact upon his experience. How does the built environment shape people's *psyche*, and what are the ways of countering the detrimental psychological effects of living in a metropolis?

The experiment was part of research on the atypical brains of London's black cab drivers, whose posterior region of their hippocampus is significantly denser compared to, for instance, bus drivers who drive fixed routes. This increased posterior hippocampal grey matter volume is acquired in response to increased taxi driving experience. It is not known whether this increased navigational ability is due to an increased volume of cells, or if this is caused by more connections between brain cells. Any type of activity has an effect on the molecular structure of our nervous system, and thus has long-lasting consequences for our lives. The volume increases with years of experience. Drivers of black cabs are special because, unlike colleagues across the world, they have to learn London's 25,000 streets by heart rather than relying on GPS. The result is an extraordinary spatial memory, and a detailed mental map of London. We wanted to know if the writer, an obsessive walker of London for over thirty years, had an enhanced capacity for navigation similar to the London cabbies. He did indeed. The results were literally off the map as the score fell outside the grid used for cabbies. Walking has a tremendously positive effect on your inner compass, and enhances your navigational skills.

Portraits of My Brain Just After the Attack

But now it's my turn to be MRI'd and this time it isn't a scientific experiment. This is undeniably real. An assistant, the source of whose irritation is unknown to me, is asking me to lie on the stretcher, and in broken English is taking me through the process. He tells me that the doctor leading the scan is Docteur Paradis. I like irony, even of the cosmic variety, but this is getting a tad too much. Maybe it's his stage name? I comply and lie down, my head on the block, earmuffs on to reduce the racket and an emergency button in case I freak out. The scanner creates a powerful electromagnetic field that will re-align the protons of the water molecules in my head, revealing diseased or dead tissue. There's an incredible noise. Its sound reminds me of industrial rock from the early nineties: Nine Inch Nails, and Ministry – the drone that I used to dance to in Amsterdam squats until the sun came up.

Lying in the machine, earmuffs on, my eyes closed, I listen to the French voices shouting commands over the speaker. The scan itself takes twenty minutes but feels much longer. I'm surprised claustrophobia isn't getting the better of me.

Rosencrantz and Guildenstern take me back to the comforts of my room, this time in silence. José is there, with fresh clothes, books, my earphones. We make tea together, and we sip it slowly, talk a little. My mother and father walk into the hospital room – strange spectres, out of place. They look haggard, having driven 1,200 kilometres in one day to check up on me and provide moral support – a deeply personal, emotional journey showing their duty of care and protective instinct. It's sweet of them; I'm genuinely touched.

I am explaining to my parents what has happened in detail, what tests I have been undergoing, what the diagnosis is, and how I feel. I notice that being around just three people is exhausting. How keeping my focus on their faces whilst talking is draining. It is clear that I'm talking slowly, looking for words, and what I'm saying is causing confusion. Shakes of the head from my most intimate audience. The words don't come out right. They call for clarification, which in turn angers me. My mother, who is a big talker, is holding back for a while, but she has too many questions and, before we know it, she's unstoppable. She's nervous, understandably, doesn't know how to handle the fact that her son nearly died. I tell her to quit talking for just a moment, saying that everything needs to go slowly – very slowly. My father shuffles around in the room in silence, trying not to be there. His silence is comforting.

The neurologist enters, carrying the MRI images of my brain that are much more detailed than the CAT scans, collected in a small booklet. He tells us that I have suffered only one stroke, not two, and that the other cluster was actually the Circle of Willis, or Willis Polygon, named after the seventeenth-century English physician Thomas Willis. This is a circulatory system supplying blood to the brain. If one part of the circle is blocked or narrowed, blood flow from the other blood vessels can preserve the cerebral perfusion well enough to prevent an attack. Apparently the Willis Polygon was so dense on the CT image that it looked like it had burst. A fortunate misdiagnosis.

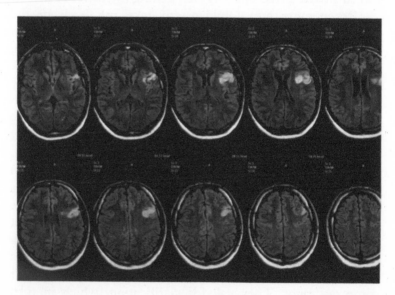

Figure 1

Portraits of My Brain Just After the Attack

José and I look at the booklet with slices through my brain; we take in these images one by one and see a white cumulus cloud growing bigger and bigger on the front part of my brain and then disappearing again, wafting away towards some unknown horizon.

It also contains twenty-four close-ups of the now dead part of my neuronal material as a bonus feature: a CD with more images – Deleted Scenes. Language is produced on the left side of the brain, my neurologist tells me, his hand gliding over the MRI image, which shows the brain in reverse. My stroke has struck in the left frontal lobe, which is the area vital for language, speech and writing. Hence my aphasia, a word derived from the Greek for speechlessness, which means literally 'no speech'. The most severe aphasia lasted twenty-four hours: for a day and night I was locked inside my body and brain that was perfectly able to think of sentences but unable to utter them. Below the frontal lobe, towards the front side of the brain, is Broca's Area, discovered by the nineteenth-century doctor, anatomist and anthropologist Paul Broca. Broca's Area sits next to the one that controls the muscle activity of the tongue and mouth, which is involved in forming spoken words. Broca deduced this with the help of his patient, Louis Leborgne, who could understand language perfectly well but was unable to speak. He had no motor problems with his tongue, mouth or vocal cords. He would whistle and was able to hum a tune but he could not sing words.

Just towards the back, in the posterior region of the left frontal lobe, lies Wernicke's Area, discovered by neurologist and psychologist Carl Wernicke in the late nineteenth century, which is responsible for recognizing and understanding words. Given my inability to pronounce difficult words while still being able to read my Murakami novel, it is evident that the infarct struck closer to the Broca than the Wernicke area. I can write in my head, but not on paper nor on a screen.

The neuroscientist explains that the flows of information through my brain structures are disrupted or blocked completely. The language processes flow from the back of the left hemisphere to the front with high-level planning and semantic processes towards the back (Wernicke) and low-level sound retrieval and articulation towards the front (Broca). The two regions are connected by a tract of fibres called the 'arcuate fasciculus', a bundle of axons (a projection from a nerve cell that conducts electrical impulses). It is like a highway with electricity running back and forth between these areas to conceive of and produce speech. In my case, the Broca area was hit, cutting off the current.

Broca   **Wernicke**

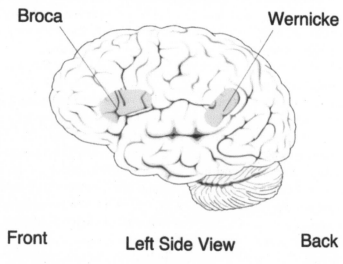

Front   **Left Side View**   **Back**

Figure 2

We talk about what might have caused the stroke. He asks about my family, whether anyone has had stroke before: the problem might be hereditary. He asks about heart problems, about thrombosis. He asks if I smoke, and I say that I smoked in my early twenties but had quit a long time ago, though I did occasionally smoke a couple of cigarettes when I went to the pub. 'No more smoking at all, ever again,' he states.

'I have something to cheer you up,' says the doctor whilst placing a chart called The Glasgow Outcome Score in my hands. It describes the outcome in patients with head trauma, giving a rough idea of how a patient is doing without drilling down to the specific reason why. The chart has five Scores:

The Glasgow Outcome Score

Score	Description
1	Death
2	Persistent vegetative state: patient exhibits no obvious cortical function
3	Severe disability (conscious but disabled): patient depends on others for daily support as a result of mental or physical disability or both
4	Moderate disability (disabled but independent): patient is independent as far as daily life is concerned; the disabilities found include varying degrees of dysphasia, hemiparesis or ataxia, as well as intellectual and memory deficits and personal changes
5	Good recovery: resumption of normal activities, although there may be minor neurological or psychological deficits

'At the moment you are in category 4 but there is no reason not to assume that with some therapy and sensible lifestyle adjustments you will make it to category 5,' says the brain doctor. 'Get in touch with your GP. You need to take it easy during your recovery.' His caring voice changes to that of a detective: 'We need to know why this happened; we need to determine the aetiology.' I like this. I need an explanation, a cause – the culprit must be unveiled. He explains we'll do two tests: the brain today, tomorrow the heart. He explains we also need to look at blood samples, find out if my cholesterol is too high. Staff will investigate my arteries. Another doctor will conduct an echocardiogram to see if there is any abnormality that could have caused my stroke. We must find out what's gone wrong in my head. I need to know, because we might be able to discover how to prevent another one in the future. The next stroke is likely to kill me.

The neurologist leaves and in my lap is the booklet with brain images. The images strike me as utterly clinical and rational – what am I to do with them? What do these images of my brain mean? What do they mean *to me*? Next to the images I see the name of the victim printed as well as today's date but, despite these facts, it doesn't feel like I'm looking at my head. There seems to be an irreconcilable chasm between the objective, irreducible truth that these MRI images convey and my own emotional experience.

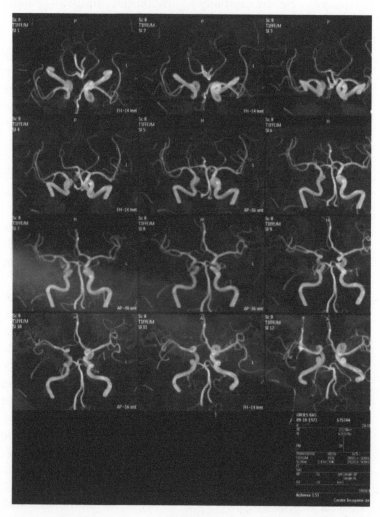

Figure 3

Portraits of My Brain Just After the Attack

And I know I should be distrustful of MRI images. During the memory project and my work with neuroscientists, many of my literary colleagues and I have been critical of the way in which neuroscientists produced and interpreted them. The ability to control the 3D image and slice through someone's brain also seems to trigger a sense of control over, and explanation of, brain processes, whilst the complexity of those processes makes the human brain still a mystery. A science journalist had warned that there was a dangerous gap between the colourful map composed out of MRI images and the complex territory of the actual brain itself. This journalist warned against the fetishization of MRI images, which seemed implicitly to promise control over an organ that is entirely enigmatic.

Again José and I browse the sets of stills that evidence the impact of the stroke on the left hemisphere: clusters of wiry, white tunnels, dead nerves, deprived of oxygen. They look like distracted doodles made by someone chatting distractedly on the phone. We need to reframe these images to make sense of them. We decide to retitle them *Portraits of My Brain Just After the Attack.*

The cloud on the photos, a strange mist that seems to be coming and going, is not a phenomenon that arrives and leaves: as the 'photos' slice through my brain, what I'm seeing is a still image of low-lying fog that will not go away, never. I notice I'm using metaphors – what the images really show are sections of small vessels in my brain that have died and turned white: localised micro-starvation, showing up as a white cloud of fog. Ironically enough, after the first pain of the stroke had subsided, it did indeed feel like a fog in my mind.

We suddenly see a curious beauty in the images. The rows and rows of these black-and-white slices of my brain compare to pop art by Andy Warhol. They are not embodiments of truth about ordinary experience but point to a division, the explanatory gap between lived experience and the operations of the brain inside my skull.

A friend calls them 'crazy squiggly squiggles'. A novelist

friend, who has a long-standing interest in geology, defines them differently: 'Intriguing coils, Bas. They look like fulgurites, bolts of lightning in your brain. Is that illuminated spot on the first photo the attack?' A fulgurite is a hollow tube of molten rock or sand which is created by the intense heat of a lightning strike. I tell her I like the idea that the cells in my brain fired too intensely and that the extreme heat created a short-circuit, burning a clump of cells to death.

Portraits of My Brain Just After the Attack is tangible evidence of the fact that something had gone wrong in my head. They are comforting, as they could be clues to understanding what and why this had happened – photographic stills acting as objective markers of control. And somehow, the more I look at the images, the more they seem to become oracular, as if they were not about my present self but are predicting my future. The images are becoming an endless swirl of *memento mori*, the Latin phrase that reminds us to remember that we will one day die.

I realise that, just as in Joyce's epiphany, the MRI pictures are *images* and not the real thing. And I have just appropriated these images creatively to reinterpret them. This gives me power. Art and culture enable me to make sense of my stroke.

In the evening, José departs for our holiday home. I'm exhausted, lying in my hospital bed feeling useless. Nurses bring me my food while the blood pressure monitor keeps squeezing my arm. I had hoped that French hospital food would be *exquise*. I fancied a cassoulet and a cheese platter, but I'm getting a watery carrot soup and some *légumes* and mashed *pommes de terre*. They taste of nothing, part of the regime of desensitization. A nurse checks the stats and notes that I'm doing okay but that my blood pressure still needs to come down. Another bowl of watery carrot soup will do the trick, definitely, I think. She takes away the food tray. I watch some French television, but all these people talking at speed in a strange language exhaust me. I look at the Murakami novel on the bedside table, but I've had enough fiction for one day. I just lie here, all alone, trying not to think about the implications of what's happened. A nurse comes into my room and chats to me whilst checking my blood pressure and heartbeat. She turns off the light when she leaves. It is dark, now. I mark this day as over, an act that I imagine gives me control over my immediate experience these past few days. But another shock rushes towards me: I will have to mark a particular part of my life as over. My slow, tired thoughts are drifting off, longing for blissful coma. I must sleep. If I go under long and deep perhaps I can sleep this nightmare off.

Chapter Three
The **PHILIPS** Phenomenon

The next day, after another disappointing breakfast, Rosencrantz appears with an old-fashioned, rickety wheelchair and pushes me through the corridors in silence. Some doors in the stroke unit are open and I see a white-haired woman sitting in her bed, staring into the distance, muttering to herself. Despite our age difference, she's a fellow victim, we're united by the same affliction.

To get to the building where a doctor will investigate the flow of blood in my neck we have to go through a courtyard outside. I have been in the hospital for nearly forty-eight hours, and the sunlight is overpowering, even at this early time of day. But it is the smells that are triggering all sorts of sensations: I smell blossom, dust, something sweet which refuses to be named, and a hint of cigarette smoke. My senses are overloaded. I speculate that my hospital room is a sensory deprivation tank of sorts but without the hallucinations.

I'm parked next to an elderly man and manage to get across a rudimentary message. That I am from *des Pays-Bas... Je vis à Londres. Je suis professeur... de littérature anglaise.* I want to continue with *J'ai eu.... un accident vasculaire cerebral* but this is way too difficult for my mouth. I point to my head. This elderly man, from what I can make out, has suffered a heart attack. To me he seems a bit too cheerful, his creaking voice full of life and gratitude. He puts his hand on my arm and squeezes it gently. He tells me that I shouldn't look so solemn; I should enjoy life. I tell him I'll try to but that I've planned a Big Career for myself. He tuts, says, '*Non, non, non, mon ami...* You must enjoy life while you can!' It's probably sound advice but I'm thirty-nine, still relatively young, and want to leave my mark. I have my Big Career to consider, *mon vieux*, I think.

I meet the technician, a guy with a droopy face; he's grumpy and does not speak English. He gestures a lot, showing me a grey stick that he'll slide along my neck. He points to the probe, which lies on a cart attached to a TV monitor. He smears gel on my neck and presses the cold probe onto my skin below which, as the black-and-white image on the monitor shows, blood is pumping enthusiastically through my carotid artery. 'Very good,' he observes.

After this scan I must fast until the echocardiogram commences in the afternoon. I read some more Murakami but I'm lacklustre, down about my predicament. My parents are walking around the town doing things that tourists do. José hangs about and drinks tea in silence. We had planned to be at the Toulouse-Lautrec Museum in Albi today. We both love post-impressionism and are fascinated by the strange, tragic life of Toulouse-Lautrec, an aristocrat turned painter who never fitted into mainstream society because a genetic disease stunted his growth. He suffered many health problems throughout his life, turned to the bottle, contracted syphilis, and died at the age of thirty-six. He painted over 700 canvasses, nearly 300 watercolours, and produced more than 5,000 drawings. His contorted figures and the multi-perspectival configurations squeezed together in the frames reflect his less-than-normal position in society.

Like Toulouse-Lautrec, I was now disabled. I wondered how the effects of the stroke would impact on my life, on my position in society. Would I too see the world and myself differently? Weirdly, I was excited by the prospect.

José makes more phone calls, explaining the situation to her mother and my sister- and brother-in-law; she's texting our friends. People are shocked; there is great concern for me, and this wave of compassion feels heart-warming. And I am shocked too by the realisation of my mortality, which has been announced so overwhelmingly. And embarrassed also. As if I should be ashamed of my brain infarct. Like I've done this to myself.

In the afternoon, it's Guildenstern's turn to cart me through the exit. What did he say to Hamlet? *'Oh, there has been much throwing about of brains.'* It's a fascinating line because its meaning isn't directly clear but it seems to be referring to people thinking, debating, arguing.

This time we're taking a different route, to a *dépendance*. I'm introduced to the procedure by a nurse; she's the only one in the team who speaks English. She explains that this transoesophageal echocardiogram (TOE) will involve swallowing a tube, after which they will send a probe with an ultrasound transducer down my oesophagus to make images of my heart's walls and valves. The nurse tells me the TOE will be 'unpleasant' – a euphemism, I'll come to learn, for 'bloody awful'. I will be asked to gargle a gel containing an anaesthetic that numbs my mouth and tongue so that my gag reflex is suppressed, making it easier to swallow the tube.

The head of the team is talking at speed to me in a rural, southern French accent, explaining what will happen. I nod but I don't understand. The nurse is handing me the cold gel, which I put in my mouth and chew. 'Don't swallow,' she tells me, 'just chew.' My mouth goes numb. I can't feel my tongue. I must have swallowed a bit as the cold spreads to my throat and oesophagus. I want to swallow the saliva that is building up in my mouth but I can't, and it starts to drip out. Now the outside of my head as well as the inside is impaired. I want to but cannot swallow. This procedure is, I will come to learn, one of many dislocations I will experience.

They fix a mouthpiece onto my face with tape, a kind of plastic keyhole through which the tubes will enter. I have to lie on my side. Then a blue tube enters the frame. 'When she says "Yes",' the young nurse says, 'you must swallow.' I shrug my shoulders: swallowing seems a tad difficult at the moment. The blue tube enters my mouth, the doctor says 'Yes' and I try to swallow. The tube is pushed down my throat and immediately I want to vomit. 'Relax, relax,' the nurse says. 'Yes, sure,' I think, trying to breathe calmly, 'I'm doing my best, except someone is shoving a sixty centimetre long plastic tube down my throat!' I want to shout but can only blink some strange Morse code.

Water is being excreted from my tear ducts; it's not because I'm in pain, but it's pure stress that produces these tears. My instinct is to reach for the hand of the nurse; just the touch of another human being might be enough to give me the sense that everything is going to be alright. But what will these people think of me?

The TOE machine is made by Philips, a Dutch company. The name, and the old-school seventies font in which it is written – **PHILIPS** – does something to my brain. After more wriggling and twisting, the operator makes stills of my heart, but I hardly notice the discomfort anymore. I am lost in my own past, transported back to the sitting room of my family's two-up two-down where I lived until I was eleven years old. It was a youth filled with happy chapters but also troublesome episodes that forced me to escape into fictional worlds, many of which were of my own making.

Philips technology played a key role in shaping me. As I close my eyes, I see my video cassettes and the VCR into which I'm inserting them: Philips. In the mid-eighties, I'd spend hours in front of the TV. Bruce Lee's martial arts films were equally a source of fascination: *Fist of Fury, The Way of the Dragon, Enter the Dragon,* and *Game of Death. Enter the Dragon* has the most astounding ending, when the villain draws Lee into a maze of mirrors, which the Kung Fu fighter smashes to capture and kill his opponent. They inspired me to become a judoka.

I also obsessively played computer games on my Philips Videopac game computer: *Munchkin* and *Pick Axe Pete.* Yet movies were a fixation. The repetitiveness with which I watched films – including a Star Wars obsession – caused my mother to conclude that I was mildly autistic.

It wasn't a diverse cultural diet. It was mainly popular

culture, a world away from the literature, art and painting that I'd come to embrace. Perhaps I was ashamed of my background and origins in a common farmers village. I came from a family of craftsmen, teachers and entrepreneurs, was the first one to study at university and to become a scholar. At least that's what the title in front of my name indicated, though I never felt a proper academic: I considered myself a hard-working impostor. To escape from my background, I embraced Culture, 'difficult' literature from John Milton through to James Joyce, and I spent much time reading art books and visited galleries and museums. At UEA in Norwich, I held my tutorials in the Sainsbury Arts Centre and taught modernism classes in Liverpool's Walker Art Gallery, London's Courtauld Institute of Art and the National Portrait Gallery.

Looking back, I realise I overcompensated in order to reject my past self. But this involuntary trip to my past makes me wonder how the stroke and its effects will give me a different perspective on life and on the world. I mostly wonder, how I will be changed? From pop culture to punk rocker to academic – what's next? The thought fills me with trepidation and excitement at the same time.

Philips shaped my youth even further. My father bought a Philips video camera, which I used to make my own movies. With a battery weighing three kilos strapped to my back I'd shoot fictional scenarios in which my friends would act. When I was sixteen, I made a ten-minute detective film starring my sister and, at seventeen, a short drama with my gymnastics' buddies. I also worked for the regional TV station, covering local events, such as the infamous Swamp Marathon, in which a hundred or so local contestants raced across the soggy meadowlands and braved the slimy water of ditches whilst uncaring cows looked on.

My dad used the camera to tape my performances at gymnastics tournaments. I had a knack for this most elegant of sports. The tangy odours of the practice hall, sweaty and rubbery, the feeling of the dry magnesium powder, and the chemical smell of the rubber blocks of foam in the 'pit' in which we landed during practice – these sensations were all coming back to me, here in the hospital room. Hands caked in white, my grips made of leather to prevent blisters, often covered in blood. I worked hard, training three, four days a week, competing in matches across the Netherlands. I excelled. In the late eighties I came third in the national championships, twice in a row. I had two lives, one as an athlete, and another as a high-school student whose results were suffering. At the height of my career, I was scouted for the Dutch Olympics team.

The injuries came inevitably: my back gave way, my left Achilles tendon become permanently inflamed. There were lapses of concentration, more physical harm. When dismounting the high bar with a double somersault I let go too late and landed with my shins on the steel, after which I couldn't walk for days. Then as now my body's limits were responsible for changing the course my life was taking, and I wondered how this new insult to my bodily fitness would alter my life journey.

I was forced to quit sport and my life took a different turn. I discovered girls, clubs, cigarettes, The Pixies, Nirvana, guitars. Half a year later, I had eyebrow and lip piercings, was playing in an indie band, smoking joints, chasing and being chased by tattooed girls and boys.

But my own beating heart on the Philips monitor reminds me of another image: a heart *not* beating. This black-and-white image on the Philips machine is a reminder of death, of loss. Four years ago, when José was pregnant for the second time, we went for the twelve-week scan, thinking that everything was fine. We were overjoyed that our perseverance was rewarded with a beautiful baby daughter, Lotte, after we'd lost our earlier pregnancy of Dagmar. So much pain, time, emotions, tears were now finally, finally bearing fruit. Our *kindje*, our child, was about to show itself on the monitor, with a beating heart.

When the hands of the sonographer let the transducer glide over José's swollen belly nothing appeared. We expected to see the contours of our tiny baby but we just saw white noise. No heartbeat – nothing. The sonographer broke the news: the foetus had died weeks earlier.

There were no words to describe the sorrow we felt. At that moment, a large part of us died in that room, together with our baby. Our imagined future changed completely in that one moment: no longer were we to be parents, supporting our children in their education, teaching them how to be nice people and taking them on holidays to Indonesia to show them their roots. José wouldn't breastfeed Lotte, and we wouldn't take her to her first day at school, nor support her in her tennis finals, nor sing with her in our family band. All those fantasies were brutally wiped in that moment. We'd dreamt one day we'd be grandparents, looking back upon our successful lives with gratitude and pride. Now, the future was empty.

I look at the Philips monitor once again. The black-and-white screen reminds me of one thing only, I now understand: death.

Now that these personal memories are awoken from a concrete bunker somewhere in my mind, I find my past not only traumatic but also irresistibly disarming: I'm charmed by this young boy who was so ambitiously trying to make a career in film for himself. I'm proud of the discipline of my former top athlete self that has stood me in good stead ever since. And the memories of Dagmar and Lotte – they're still too much too bear, but I also understand that I've come a long way in coping with the grief.

What just happened to me is a version of the famous 'madeleine moment' in Marcel Proust's monumental memory project, *In Search of Lost Time*. Proust narrates his childhood and adolescent experiences and the way in which they have shaped his character. The first volume of the novel, *Swann's Way*, contains the famous passage that demonstrates Proust's theory of 'involuntary' memory. This is different from voluntary memory, which happens when you consciously recall a specific event in the past. In Proust's novel, the middle-aged narrator is thinking back to his youth, and reconstructing his life according to his memories. But something odd happens when he dips a madeleine cake into his lime-blossom tea: there is a sudden rush of memories from his childhood in Combray. Proust remembers the old grey house, the city square, the flowers in his family's garden: 'all of this which is assuming form and substance, emerged, town and garden alike, from my cup of tea'.

This event has come to be known as the 'Proust Phenomenon', which is the fact that odours are better cues in triggering autobiographical memories than the perceptions of the other senses. I'd become an expert in understanding this phenomenon with a number of Memory Network experiments I had organised and designed. I'd shown that we are able to remember images better if they are associated with strong smells such as garlic or lemon. And I and a psychologist also designed experiments to show that there are specific location-bound smells and memories: odours that belong to a certain area, which are also associated with a kind of collective memory of a community. In a West Midlands region of the UK known as the Black Country – because of the heavy industry it was home to until recently – smells including burnt rubber, faggots and Teddy Grays (a locally produced herbal tablet) were identified better by the local population than by outsiders.

But lying there in the hospital with that tube worming around in my gut, I understand that reading about someone else's memories being triggered is nothing compared to true-life experience. The rushing back of my own childhood memories is infinitely stronger, emotionally.

My memory prompt is not a smell, but a word – a sign, or logo – that is opening up parts of my past I thought I'd forgotten, or plot points if you will, that have been formative in shaping who I am. But the shock of the stroke event and the invasion of my body by this medical team and their instruments have also brought back many episodes from my childhood and youth. They feel pleasant, these unexpected snapshots, even though some are painful. Over the past year, I have been focused on the present and the future, most of the time looking ahead to work on strategies for my Big Career, setting goals, deadlines and milestones. I haven't looked back a lot.

'Your heart is very good,' the doctor tells me. She gives me two thumbs up. The probe and camera are retracted and the tube is taken out of my oesophagus. The mouthpiece is released and I'm lying on my back again. My face feels strange: I can only half-feel my lips, am unable to swallow, but I am weirdly happy nonetheless.

When I'm back in my private room, José and my parents are there to greet me. We talk about the nasty procedure I've just endured, and we chat for a bit. I'm talking slowly, looking for words, but what I'm saying is also causing confusion. The words don't come out right. A bit later, José and my parents again depart for our holiday home. The Murakami novel on the bedside table lies patiently beside me but I cannot be bothered to read. The clock on the wall opposite is ticking away time, time I will never be able to retrieve.

Chapter Four
How Are You Getting Back?

On the morning of my third day in hospital I am discharged. This is standard procedure. There are some final check-ups, and the neurologist gives me instructions. The stay has also been good for my hernia, which has virtually disappeared, the result of seventy-two hours of bedrest. I'm skinnier and my broken mind feels rested and clear, somehow, but I'm afraid of leaving the security of the hospital, the care of the nurses and doctors. The world beyond the safe, white walls of the hospital scares me.

José and my parents arrive, and they chat. I listen, wearily. The neurologist comes in and takes the time to speak to my parents; he assures them that everything will be alright. He writes a prescription. The NHS covers the bill, which will be sent to me in the post as well. We're done.

Outside, the light hurts my eyes. I'm flabbergasted. I've been indoors for seventy-two hours but already the world seems altogether different. It's only been three days yet I seem to have lost my connection with the light, air, the sounds and smells of the outside world. Living life is a habit. Our routines ensure we don't have constantly to adjust our bodies and minds. They preserve biological energy, so to submit to custom pays off. Consciousness is a protective shield that defends us against the overwhelmingly sensory bombardment that is the world. Rational, logical thinking is hard, and so is art and the critical faculty it engages. One of the great things about contemplating other people's creative expression is that it challenges our routines. Art is the great disruptor.

For a moment, standing at the hospital gates, I enjoy the Mediterranean warmth on my face and body, feel the breeze touch my skin, and I imagine this has all been an unsettling dream, a particularly vivid nightmare. But I'm afraid of being responsible for myself again, of the freedom that awaits me – a skinny liberty. I want to go to the Toulouse-Lautrec museum, immerse myself in the mysterious viscous world of the painter's work or visit the cathedral, but we can't: I have to buy my medicine. I'm irritated by these mundane activities, waiting my turn in line, sedated by the chemical drugstore smell. My old life – I want to step back into it as soon as possible.

At noon, we walk to Le Clos Sainte-Cécile, a restaurant named after the famed Albi cathedral, where we get a spot in the sunny garden. I order sparkling water, and, raising a glass, I say: '*À votre santé!*' To your health. We chat about the implications of my neuronal blockade. I want to make sure that everyone has a good time, that all feel at home, as an apology for dragging them into this alarming situation. I want to speak a few words, but my mother delivers a monologue, until she's overtaken by José – one of the characteristics the closest two women in my life share is their penchant for hyperlocution. My father is silent at first but is also wondering, like a practical Dutchman, how I will make the journey back to London. I get agitated quickly. Too many brains are sparking too excitedly in this lovely French garden where the sun is shining too hard and too many voices are producing too much noise. After lunch, José suggests we visit the cathedral but I'm exhausted by the sensory impressions and I want to go back to our holiday home to sleep.

The next few days are sluggish. Or, rather, I am sluggish. We mostly just hang around the house doing nothing, plagued by worry at the back of our minds. My mum and dad announce that they will head home the next day; they have business to take care of. I thank them for their concern and presence, apologise for being cantankerous. I sense they feel uncomfortable because I'm tetchy.

Work starts to creep in. I do a video call with my line manager and agree that my teaching load is be cut and that I will let go of a few Ph.D. students. Everyone is concerned about me, including the University's higher management. Their worry touches me but I also get the acute sense that I'm being watched by my bosses. This is quite ironical: I need to teach only one course, *Poetics of Surveillance*, a specialist module that traces how literature has represented forms of observation throughout history, from the all-seeing eye of God in the Bible to the effects of social media in the twenty-first century. It starts in three weeks' time but I need to have a health check before I am allowed to teach again. I catch up on my emails; that is, I read them but avoid writing them to prevent embarrassment and confrontation with my predicament. A sudden rush: I am *disabled*, a word that stabs me like a cold knife.

How disabled am I? On the web I find the Modified Rankin Scale, dating from 1957, which is the scale that neurologists and researchers often use to categorize stroke patients:

Modified Rankin Scale

Score	Description
0	No symptoms at all
1	No significant disability despite symptoms; able to perform all usual duties and activities
2	Slight disability; unable to perform all previous activities but able to look after own affairs without assistance
3	Moderate disability; requiring some help but able to walk without assistance
4	Moderate severe disability; unable to walk without assistance and unable to attend to own bodily needs without assistance

5   Severe disability; bedridden, incontinent, and
       requiring constant nursing care and attention
6   Death

The Rankin Scale charts the decreasing ability to function independently. What the scale really maps for me, though, is freedom: it measures physical autonomy or the level of need for outside help in daily life, your level of independence. At the moment I'm somewhere between 1 and 2. I can perform all physical activities, except for speaking properly.

Being able to put myself into a box that describes my physical liberty creates a sense of power. The idea that I can objectively place myself on some sort of scale is comforting – it distances my self from my trauma. My experience becomes abstract and I feel like a statistic. It helps to lessen my worry, to keep me calm. But I'm also aware that my stroke will have an effect not only on my body but also on my mental and social life. I sense there will be psychological impact and a change in my relationships with friends and family, my job. I feel anxious and cut off from the world. Is there a scale to measure the psychological impact as well? My personal experience seems much less easy to categorise. Mentally I feel adrift.

Early the next day my parents leave after we thank them for their support. In the morning, José and I lounge on the terrace of the farmhouse, breakfasting and reading. We decide it might be relaxing to go for a picnic in the countryside. This time José drives. We discuss my stroke and how this will affect my work and life. We talk about whether we should perhaps attempt to keep it quiet within the academic community, but my mother and José think that's impossible given the level of writing and speaking impairment. It's also not desirable, as my work and the NHS will be able to offer support to get me through this ordeal in the best way possible. My future is full of questions.

It's a beautiful day, still very hot, though the summer heat is tempering. There's a hint of autumn in the wind, with clouds throwing shadows once in a while. We find a pleasant, sheltered spot in a field tucked away in the rolling hills that stretch as far as the eye can see. We're not saying much. The silence is heavily meaningful. Neither of our lives seems to have worked out the way we imagined. I feel such a failure.

We have bought bubbly from a local delicatessen, a tomato salad and local cheeses, bread. I sit motionless on our blanket, head thrown back, feeling loved by the sun whose rays gently touch my skin and by the sparkle of bubbles that hit the roof of my mouth, slightly acidic, ticklish – how can liquid feel so dry? My senses seem sharper, overwhelmed even.

Philosophers and neuroscientists call such basic sensory stimuli *qualia*: the awareness of subjective sensations such as the taste and smell of a swig of wine with certain notes and tones, the feeling of tropical rain on your face (touch, sounds, taste and smell), a toothache (pain registered by a connection of nerves that runs between your mouth and your brain), or the colours in a Yayoi Kusama painting. You can only experience qualia; they are sensations that are very difficult to put into words.

Sitting here in this French meadow I'm reminded of a passage from Edith Wharton's *Ethan Frome*, in which the young Frome describes his romantic feelings for his wife's cousin, Mattie:

> [...] there were other sensations, less definable but more exquisite, which drew them together with a shock of silent joy: the cold red of sunset behind winter hills, the flight of cloud-flocks over slopes of golden stubble, or the intensely blue shadows of hemlocks on sunlit snow. When she said to him once: 'It looks just as if it was painted!' it seemed to Ethan that the art of definition could go no farther, and that words had at last been found to utter his secret soul...

Ethan and Mattie share this epiphany: just as this young, beautiful woman sets his senses and the surrounding landscape ablaze, her 'spirit had trembled with the same touch of wonder'. Wharton's novel also shows that great literature is able to capture qualia in carefully chosen words – they roughly translate sensory experiences into meaning. That's the power of good writing.

I want to cry at realising the sheer pleasure of having survived my stroke, of still being able to *be here*. I manage to fight back the tears and utter: 'It's... to be alive, you know, the sheer miracle of... life... it's just...' I'm not even close to formulating a proper sentence.

My mobile phone rings, destroying my reverie, and I'm back in the French meadow. It's my GP, asking, 'How are you getting back?' He's rung me to discuss what's been happening over the past few days. If strokes run in my family? Negative. Some issues with the heart, with some long-term prescriptions for beta-blockers.

'How am I getting back?' A loaded question. He's asking how I'll cross the geographical distance from the south of France to London, but I hear questions about recovery. Can I get back to where I was before – to whom I was before?

Sure, I want to get back, but I'm no longer sure I actually can. I long for my London home and the safety of my study. I built my own bookcases for my study, the best room in the flat, cosy and warm, a hiding place from the world, shielded by walls of books. Whilst I worked away at my desk, reading and writing, José would be reading in a rocking chair. Those were the grand productive days: I was young, organised conferences, ran a series on contemporary writers, and published five books in the space of three years. That life seems to have slipped away forever.

José and I spend our last few days in France trying to re-establish our routine: eat, read, walk, explore, sleep. We drive to an independent vineyard that makes Gaillac wines, a place we've been coming to for a few years. We chat to the owner, who complains about business just like he did last time. We did this before, the trip and the conversation. Repeating this ritual feels familiar, comfortable.

José needs to go back to Amsterdam: her holiday, which has been far from relaxing, is over. Weird: for a moment I was under the impression that we still lived together and that we'd drive back to London together. My *psyche* has the urge to reunite us. But the reality is that we lead different lives in different countries. The realisation shocks me. Once again she's been by my side at an important, life-changing moment: studying English literature, supporting my band, emigrating to the United Kingdom, both achieving degrees together, getting married in Venice, experiencing the loss of our pregnancies together. And now the stroke, which has drawn us closer again. We feel so intimate; our lives intertwined for so long. I want to ask her to come back with me to London – I'm afraid – but she needs to go back to Holland. It means that I will have to spend my recovery by myself.

To break up the journey back home we visit my friend, an English writer who lives in the Loire valley. The drive to Dolus-le-Sec is arduous, a sick nightmare, rolling ceaselessly up and down hills whilst dark grey skies cry. José drives most of the journey but I do a chunk also and I'm broken when we arrive. My friend is curious about my condition and asks me questions in a voice whose fluency irks me; I try to answer, slowly. Whilst José and my friend prepare food, joking and chatting, I'm sitting slumped at the kitchen table, simply staring at these perfect creatures whose speech flows forth from their mouths without any problems.

The next day we drive to Paris and I drop José off at the Gare du Nord. It is a hard goodbye, as all of our many farewells have been over the past few years since our relationship break. Our caresses and kisses take minutes. She tells me to take good care of myself, and that she'll come over very soon. I watch her slip away between the train-station doors and I feel bereft.

On to Calais, to the ferry which will take me back to my adopted homeland. A three-and-a-half-hour drive, alone for the first time since my stroke, and by the time I get to the harbour I feel depleted. An emptiness is growing in my gut. Waiting in line at border control, I check myself in the rear-view mirror to find a grey, undead face. I don't recognize myself. But the man in the booth, looking at the picture of me in my passport, does.

The *Pride of Britain* ferry is chock-full with tourists and truck drivers. I stand on the aft deck with them, belonging to neither group. Sea gulls cry for food against the dark grey sky. Dads are pointing towards the horizon whilst talking to their kids, and mums are shivering in the open sea wind. My back turned to England, I watch the continent disappear.

I'm not a man who doesn't cry, but it's been a while: after the second miscarriage we suffered and the prospect of childlessness, I could cry no longer – the well of sorrow was dry. Now, involuntarily, tears flood down, tears of fear and tears of surprise at the violence of life, and tears for life's unfairness. This year is my *annus horribilis*, I realise. All the things I have built up over the past twenty years, vanished because of a minuscule blood clot.

I'm afraid of what's to come. One phrase keeps repeating itself, over and over, in my damaged head: *What the hell do I do now?*

Part II
The Art of Getting Lost

Chapter Five
Cosmic Irony

Back home in London, 'home' felt different, unfamiliar. You know the feeling when you get back to your house after a holiday and this most intimate of places feels slightly odd, not quite the way you remembered it. You've lost the close mental connection with your living room, the furniture and the photographs that you thought you knew so well, but now you just don't feel the bond. I experienced something similar but more pronounced than usual; I was keenly aware of a disconnection between my brain and my flat.

So in the first week after driving back from France, I stuck to my home. And I wanted my home to stick to me. I wrapped my most familiar space around me like a comfort blanket, trying to re-establish the relationship. The days passed slowly, time-warped. I went for walks in the neighbourhood, did some groceries and cooked, but most activities wore me out. A strange, strangely indescribable tiredness sat deep within me, and most frustratingly of all, I was unable to do anything about it.

It had been a mistake to drive from Paris to Calais and from Dover to London – over 300 miles – by myself with a broken-down brain. My awareness was fluctuating wildly: sometimes I was hyper-sensitive to my surroundings, but more often my connection to the world started to blur, dissolve and fade.

I was astounded by the way I had changed. Some changes were big, some small. For instance, I was avoiding human beings, including my closest friends. And I was starting to drink tea and was rapidly developing a keen appreciation of this magical beverage. My espresso machine stood in the corner of the kitchen, losing its Italian shine. I was afraid of any overstimulation, didn't want fully to switch on my brain. I liked the form of awareness tea generates: warm and wavy, a soft dream, not sharp and tight as coffee brings. A friend of mine had noted that tea appears to have relaxing effects, particularly in challenging situations. Tea demands respect and patience. Just after you've made it, tea will say: 'I don't think so, sucker. Take a walk around the block, and perhaps then I'll be ready for you. If I feel like it.' So, I didn't see a lot of people but I caught myself having imaginary dialogues with hot flavoured water.

My writing was still abominable:

Dear Suzanne,
I hope all's well.
Thank you very much for you're concurn about me conditton, its greet to now that so many of your lookinout fo me its great to feek lovedbysmy poelp...

I stopped. This was too frustrating to cope with.

I also did something stupid. Overwhelmingly and abundantly available and seductive, the technology that surrounds us pretty much everywhere makes it so easy to stumble on stuff you don't want to know, don't want to see. Being of a curious disposition, I was searching online for the life expectancy for young stroke victims. I found an article on recent research with the sobering headline 'Higher Mortality for Young Stroke Survivors'. The results were depressing. The research had been conducted by scientists with a sense of humour that was dark as a moonless night. The project was called 'Follow-Up of Transient Ischemic Attack and Stroke Patients and Unelucidated Risk Factor Evaluation: FUTURE'. But it turned out that the future of young stroke victims is severely compromised, statistically. They have a significantly greater risk of dying prematurely, according to these neuroscientists. Neurons were firing away, making small explosions go off in my head, when I read:

> Individuals who suffered a stroke between the ages of 18 and 50 years had significantly poorer 20-year survival when compared with the general population in the Netherlands, with death rates more than twice as high as expected.
>
> After surviving the first year, patient death rates trended upward, with elevated risk continuing for several decades.
>
> The researchers found that the cumulative 20-year mortality risk was 24.9 percent for patients with TIA; 26.8 percent for patients with ischemic stroke; and 13.7 percent for patients with hemorrhagic stroke. Analysis of the data indicated that after surviving the first 30 days after ischemic stroke, the cumulative mortality tracked higher than expected, based on nationwide mortality data.
>
> The cumulative 20-year mortality for ischemic stroke among 30-day survivors was higher in men than in women (33.7 percent vs. 19.8 percent).

I couldn't really read and absorb this article coherently. 'Twice as high as expected'. 'Trending upward'. I panicked. This confirmed my death sentence. I wouldn't live a full life; there was a high chance that one morning I wouldn't wake up, or that I would collapse in front of 150 students during a lecture. I was in the worst category, the male ischaemic stroke survivor. There's a one-third chance that my brain would glitch again within the next 20 years, most likely with a deadly outcome.

It was depressing and I wasn't sure how to cope with these hard cold facts. Should I keep calm and carry on as usual, stoically? Or did I have to change my lifestyle, and let go of my voracious, uncompromising attitude to life? Would I have to become more sensible, take on less work, less play, quit my band, start behaving like a responsible adult? Yuk. The very thoughts repelled me.

Random facts were everywhere, but their objectivity failed to calm me down because they contained seriously distressing news. Maybe I should have been drinking more milk and eating even more cheese in the past: research suggested that an increment of 200 grams of milk decreases the risk of stroke by 7%. From 25 grams of cheese a day you also reduce the risk of brain damage. But rather than comforting me, and giving a sense of control, my research into neuroscience unearthed all sorts of facts that I didn't want to know.

My investigations into my own private brain attack had started – unbeknownst to myself – a couple of years before the stroke occurred. I'd been leading a group, The Memory Network, a bunch of writers, critics and scientists investigating how memory was changing in the twenty-first century. The brain had a starring role in the research. We were interested in the implications of a population that suffers from diseases of the ageing brain, like Alzheimer's and dementia. Our team investigated how a tiny neural structure called the olfactory bulb (a small organ in the brain, close to the nose) was able to conjure up highly emotional childhood memories when sniffing an odour we hadn't smelled in a while. We also researched the effects of GPS technology on the brain's natural navigational skills.

Whilst recovering from my stroke, one of these colleagues remarked: 'Well, the willingness to suffer a stroke shows your unconditional devotion to the cause of the memory project.' The cosmic irony (as one friend called it with a sense of drama) of my brain attack wasn't lost on me. I had become my own case study. My brain had volunteered myself to explore a stroke.

Alone in my flat, I started thinking about the relationship that our society has with the brain. Perhaps this was an attempt to grasp my situation and try to get on with my job as lecturer. Over the past few decades, the dense clump of cells that we carry around, weighing just over a kilogram, has received an incredible amount of attention, and not only from the experts who study the brain. Since the decade of the brain in the 1990s, we have been witness to an increasing emphasis on the value of scientific research into the subject. Similar to the mapping of the human genome craze in the 1980s, research is obsessively focused on understanding the brain, as if this could solve all major individual biological problems, or even collective social ones. The neuroscientist Dick Swaab, a fellow Dutchie, started his book *We Are Our Brains* as follows:

> Everything we think, do and refrain from doing is determined by the brain. The construction of this fantastical machine determines our potential, our limitations and our characters; *we are our brain*. Brain research is no longer confined to looking for the cause of brain disorders; it also seeks to establish why we are as we are. It is a quest to find ourselves.

Swaab's opening salvo is a provocatively utopian claim that underestimates how your upbringing and socio-cultural context determine the formation of your character. He is nodding towards neuroscientist Joseph LeDoux's controversial claim in *The Synaptic Self* that 'You are your synapses', by which LeDoux meant that human identity is to a large extent shaped by how your brain works.

But the object of neuroscience had shifted from understanding the brain itself to explaining the very nature of human beings. The foundational belief of this neuromania was that new insights into the functioning of the human brain would lead not only to novel possibilities of techno-scientific intervention but to a radical transformation of our sense of what it is to be human – without involving other fields such as psychology, sociology, philosophy and what have you. Just as James Joyce set out to write the 'uncreated conscience' of the Irish, neuroscientists seem to want to master the nature of the human race – without realising that their *modus operandi* is incomplete on its own. Some people working in the humanities and social sciences felt threatened, as it was their job to explain the nature of humans.

I saw it more as an exciting opportunity for collaboration because I knew that literature is often the first to point out phenomena, such as the Proust Phenomenon. But I was also aware that Bram Stoker's *Dracula* contains a theory about the role of pheromones (the chemical compounds that the human body secretes) in sexual attraction for women. The quotation from Swaab suggests that brain disease – or the brain not functioning properly – is a key to understanding humans. The writer Susan Sontag had already argued this decades ago in *Illness as Metaphor*: illness is knowledge, she stated, and failing health can bring us much knowledge about how humans work – or don't. Even earlier, a century ago, the German writer Thomas Mann also proclaimed that understanding disease can be used to gain insight into the functioning of people: 'There is no deeper knowledge without the experience of disease and all heightened healthiness must be achieved by the route of illness.' I saw a pattern whereby literature was often the first to point out something important about our world.

I also realised that there was something religious about the focus on disease: from all of them, writers and neuroscientists alike, malady and suffering were the road to wisdom. Their logic fitted into the Judeo-Christian tradition, whose sway is far from over, perhaps unconsciously. And whereas these (mostly male) neuroscientists presented themselves as the pinnacle of rationality, I saw a kind of God Complex manifest itself in their emphases. Some neuroscientists seem to present themselves as saviours of mankind – great redeemers who bring salvation – human gods in whose naïve enthusiasm I detected hubris. In neuroscientific work there seems to be a tendency towards an over-confident attitude that came out of neurological positivism, which is the idea that neuroscientists can explain everything about people and society through observation of the firing neurons alone.

Undeniably the last decade had become the pinnacle of the brain era. The brain was at the height of its fame. Books and TV programmes about the brain and its (mal)functioning were everywhere. And stroke was having its moment in popular culture. In 2013, the journalist Andrew Marr had a stroke that left him partially paralysed on his left side, and he went on to present a documentary about his recovery, *Andrew Marr: My Brain and Me*. *Who Wants to be A Millionaire?* host Chris Tarrant suffered a mini-stroke on a flight from Bangkok to London in 2014. His speech was slurred and he cut down drastically on his workload. He underwent stroke rehabilitation by having to do 'bizarre exercises for months'. Since then, he too had become addicted to what he calls 'this extraordinary machine in your head'. In 2014, a Dutch woman living in north London released a Netflix documentary, *My Beautiful Broken Brain*, about her stroke that caused aphasia, leaving her unable to read, write, or speak coherently.

The brain was everywhere. Neuromania was reaching its apotheosis; (non-innate) brain injury was where it was happening, and various 'brain memoirs' were being published. My friend Jason Tougaw, an English Professor working in New York, had written on Siri Hustvedt's *The Shaping Woman*, Aliz Kates Shulman's *To Love What Is* and Jill Bolte Taylor's *My Stroke of Insight*, all autobiographical accounts of neuronal meltdowns that left them struggling with their personalities. I was starting to read some of them and the emotional turbulence they contained assured me I was in for a rough ride. My stroke had turned me into what the French philosopher Catherine Malabou had called the 'New Wounded', an 'emergent phenomenon' whereby 'victims of various cerebral lesions or attacks' and patients with degenerative brain diseases were now 'an integral part of the psychopathological landscape'. To understand what had occurred inside my skull – and why – I started to research brains and brain attacks. I already knew a bit, but I wanted and needed to know more, if I was to understand what had happened, and make some sense of my stroke.

A writer who was involved in the memory project had wished me a speedy journey towards a new normality: 'Concentrate on recovery. If you haven't already, look up "plasticity" in the brain – it will cheer you up.' Neuroplasticity was the brain's ability to adapt and change, the idea that neural pathways and synapses can alter due to changes within the body and brain. For the most part during the twentieth century, neuroscientists agreed that the brain was a static organ, and that, once it matured around one's twentieth year, that was that. This turned out not to be the case. The brain can continue to change due to many factors, from the external impact of violence to deeply traumatic emotional experiences. Although not infinitely malleable, the brain was (to a degree) mutable, adaptable, an open-ended story. Stroke survivors with disabilities could be taught to reduce their bodily impairments by, for instance, exercising afflicted limbs, which encourages brain plasticity and aids the return to normal.

My interest in plasticity had to do with my emigration to the United Kingdom and the relationship between ageing and memory. The so-called 'reminiscence bump' is a period of time between the ages of 10 and 30 (but particularly intense between the ages of 18 and 22) when we have more personal memories as these formative years help us develop a strong sense of self. During this period we experience a memory spike: the brain matures, and we experience events that shape the self; many of us start to become sexually active, leave our parental home, go to university or start our first job, meet our life partner. It's a transformative time when the brain's abilities are boosted, and we remember a high volume of autobiographical episodes from this time clearly and distinctly.

I was interested to learn that emigrants have a second memory spike: the move into a different culture and language demands that the brain restructure itself once again. New neural pathways are laid when we adapt to a different way of life and customs, and acquire another language. This neural activity ensures that these new experiences are remembered better in later life. My move to Britain with José in 2000 was the start of a second reminiscence bump – a new dense clustering of memories – and it felt like a second youth. Our time in Norwich, when we studied at the University of East

Anglia, is cauterized into our immigrant memory, incredibly vivid and detailed. Norwich was the happiest time of our lives. We had financial freedom, allowing us to use every minute of our time to work on personal growth, and we met so many interesting people. We were experiencing a second youth.

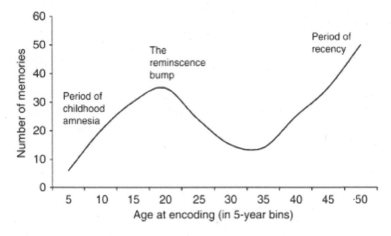

Figure 4

And now, a decade later, where was I?

I hardly recognised myself; my energetic personality had disappeared. Back home in London I had been sleeping thirteen hours a day. I slept eleven hours at night, getting into bed at 10 and waking up at 9 in the morning. I also got two hours' sleep in the afternoon, when my energy levels were dipping. I'd turned into a perpetual sleepwalker living a somnambulant nightmare.

Not only was I sleeping more – a lot more – but the nature of my nocturnal life had also changed dramatically. The boundary between waking life and sleep had become very distinct. Getting to sleep used to be a struggle. I'd lie awake for twenty or thirty minutes, going over the day's events. I have a worrying, soul-searching brain. But now, when I lay in bed, my brain would shut off immediately – unconscious within seconds. Knock-out.

And I didn't remember sleeping the next day. I had no dreams at all or, at least, I couldn't remember them. Sleep meant disappearing into the blackest darkness without any kind of consciousness. Off, out, a strange form of amnesia. Even the so-called 'default mode network', the brain regions which are active when your brain is at 'wakeful rest' (like when you are daydreaming, for instance) seemed to be switched off. Base state zero.

When I told people about my thirteen-hour sleep routine, I expected sympathetic notes about how disempowering and alienating it must have been for my behaviour to have changed so drastically. But they emailed me back, writing: 'Lucky you, I barely slept last night as the baby kept me up.' Or: 'Lucky you, my job is under threat and I sleep four hours at the moment, worried sick.' The discrepancy between the responses I'd hoped to receive and those I actually got was a chasm between me and the rest of the world that was opening up wide and fast. I was craving empathy, pity, but the world wasn't interested in other people's suffering: 'how everything turns away/Quite leisurely from the disaster', wrote W. H. Auden. In reality, this wasn't true, of course: many people cared for me – my parents, my friends, José, and my colleagues were all standing behind me. But my brain was telling me differently. The neuronal upheaval inside my head caused social disconnection as well.

I emailed a neuroscientist colleague to ask what was happening to my sleeping patterns. He told me my damaged brain was activating unused, virgin nerve cells in parts of my brain normally left untouched. Due to the lack of oxygen in the left frontal lobe of my brain, there was new activity in the surrounding area of my brain that was taking over lost functions. This is known as cortical reorganisation – re-routing. My brain was busy laying new pathways and circuits, forging new routes that would take over the tasks the dead bits of my brain could no longer carry out. This cost a lot of energy, which explained why I was so fatigued and was lacking dreams.

Neuroplasticity, I remembered. I was like a newborn child:

when you are young, your underdeveloped senses are open and easily overstimulated by light and sound, smell and taste, not yet protected by the various shields the body uses to protect itself. That childhood state was back: my mind had been reset.

Curiously, since I was usually a social creature, I'd been avoiding seeing friends, who'd first been texting me and then started ringing me, demanding an audience. I tried to fob them off with various pretexts – busy, busy – but eventually I caved in after their undeniable insistence on caring for me.

The intensity of this period after my stroke, I was to learn, was triggering a third reminiscence bump. The depth of the emotional experiences and the changes to my personality were similar to the earlier periods of transformation I had experienced – just as strong or perhaps even more powerful. So, perhaps not a death sentence but the possibility of a new life? I wondered.

A week after I was back in Old Blighty, one of my dear friends visited. She sat down with a concerned frown. She's been a friend for a long time; we share a love of music, literature and radical philosophy. She spoke quietly, distinctly. 'What was it like, the stroke? How are you feeling now?'

I felt the need to pretend that everything was going alright, so I opened a bottle of red Gaillac wine I'd brought from France. It's dark red, has a troubled look and a beautifully muddled aftertaste. We drank with abundant enthusiasm. Booze is bad for strokers, the internet had told me, because it impairs the recovery process. But I felt a need to continue patterns I was familiar with, which meant drinking just a bit too much with my friend, talking music, literature, politics and what not.

We chatted about the implications of my stroke. About everything going so slow at the moment: my moving about the room, my mangled writing that turned speaking into 'speaching'. About the teaching relief that my Head of Department was giving me. About the Occupational Health Assessment I would need to undergo at a the 'hispotal', of which I was, apparently, 'suspician'. About the blood tests, and the heart monitors. About what would happen to my life, my career.

I apologised to my friend for keeping under the radar: somehow I couldn't help but feel shame and guilt about what had happened to me. As if I somehow I was responsible for the stroke: for embracing a stressful life, for being a workaholic, for the roll-ups I smoked outside the pub, for too much thinking, too much travel, sitting too many hours on end in my desk chair, reading, writing. Perhaps I was living life too fast. Had my restlessness caught up with me?

I felt a distance between her and me and noticed, sitting in conversation in my living room, a growing self-absorption. I was becoming even more closely shackled to my inner thoughts and it didn't feel bad at all. I was experiencing an inner turn and I liked it. I wanted my friend to go away with her superior fluency of speech and her effortlessly breezing through one philosopher and writer after another.

When she was speaking, I imagined that I could feel an invisible energy field around her clever head. Brain waves. My own brain must have been emanating similar energy patterns, perhaps less intense at that moment, but it seemed as if I could feel the electrical activity of her brain impacting on my own head. The feeling was violent, intrusive – I wanted it to stop. My growing silence invited her to leave. She'd only been there for an hour. She said she understood but the expression on her face told a different story.

After dragging myself up the stairs, I watched myself brush my teeth. The man staring back at me darkly in the mirror wasn't me. The mirror seemed a tinted window on a mobster's SUV, with a view onto a shadowy underworld. I followed the movement of the brush strokes and wondered whose hand it was making them. It didn't feel like me. The normally automatic movement felt alien, as if it were the first time I was brushing my teeth. I was being squatted in by an impostor. A paralysing panic spread throughout my body and I eagerly walked towards my bedroom, towards the promise of oblivion.

Chapter Six
A Trickster in My Head

The next day, accompanied by a strapping hangover, I visited my GP. It was ten days after the accident. I waited for half an hour, trying to avoid the shouty colours of the waiting room until I was collected by my physician, a no-nonsense, don't-waste-my-time doctor, overworked, with black circles under his eyes as evidence. He politely hurried me along the corridors.

Seated at his desk he asked me – concerned eyes probing mine – how I was. I told him I felt lost and that I was worried about my tiredness, sluggishness, and that I was deep-sleeping for long periods. That I didn't feel like myself anymore; it was as if I'd been hacked by some kind of impersonator, but a damned good one. It reminded me of Capgras Syndrome, when a patient feels that someone is impersonating a close friend or family member. A trickster. A fraud. An existential squatter.

My GP was uninterested in my cerebral hacker: like a proper Gradgrindian scientist, he wanted facts. What did the neurologists in France do? What medication are you on? I showed him my *Portraits*. We discussed my work situation and he wanted to sign me off work for the standard three months, during which I must take it easy to give the recovery the best possible chance. I noted that I was being given teaching relief: instead of the usual three modules, I would only teach one. That started in less than three weeks' time. 'Is that a good idea?' he asked.

Stupidly, I formulated a response with a view to saving my career. 'Well, I really want to teach, you know, I just want to go back to normal. I can handle that. It's only three hours. My colleagues are covering other classes.'

He approved of that response. 'Fine. We'll evaluate your situation at the end of term, and in January you can go back to your normal teaching levels, if things go well, which I think they will.' This made sense.

My GP looked his watch. 'The best thing,' he told me, 'is to get on with it. Take it easy for a while and return to normal. Except you cannot drive for a month. Government regs.' I decided it was probably best not to tell him I had driven all the way back from the south of France, over 1,000 miles. 'You're making good progress.' Okay. Sure. I marched myself out of his room before he made me leave.

Even though I knew I shouldn't, I felt let down a bit. It's not that my doctor wasn't interested in my personal experience of my situation – he was, but he gave me a sense that there was nothing I could do about it. He was interested primarily in objective stuff – stuff that he could measure, like my blood pressure. I felt odd about this. I wanted some advice that also incorporated what the effects of the stroke had on my psyche. Instead, I was offered a KEEP CALM AND CARRY ON coffee mug.

Whilst walking through a park after the trip to the medical practice, the word 'trickster' buzzed around in my head. Ted Hughes's *Crow* poems came to mind. I taught *Crow* to my students on a post-war literature course. This cycle was written in the final years of the sixties, the decade when many revolutions had challenged conservative ideologies, especially about women's position in society. Organised religion was under sustained attack as well. In Hughes's poems, we meet Crow, a trickster figure from ancient mythology who uses intelligence to challenge conventional rules with a hidden agenda – to disrupt ordinary life, 'normal' conventions and overturn the 'natural' order in society. The brain is everywhere in this dark, darkly funny and deeply ironic neuropoetry, where we see a consistent attack on the idea of the soul. Modern people are left 'without souls/Dully gaping'. In 'The Black Beast',

> Crow split his enemy's skull to the pineal gland.
> [...]
> Crow crucified a frog under a microscope, he peered into
>   the brain of a dogfish.

In Hughes's vision science has triumphed, though evolution has not given us progress. The soul has departed, and the only thing we have left is the brain as the only key to explaining human beings. It's a cynical assessment of neuromania *avant la lettre*.

It doesn't mean that we've lost spirituality, though. Hughes's poems evoke ancient shamanistic processes that explore inner lives with altered states of mind. They use a continuous repetition of phrases, like a mantra that mesmerizes the audience, as if we're trapped in a nightmare of repetition, soulless and without purpose. Crow's neuro-aesthetic conjures up the apocalyptic vision of hell that we get in the medieval painter Hieronymus Bosch's *The Last Judgement*, in which people are tortured by demons. Bodies are being flayed, pierced, and heads are being stabbed. 'Crow's Account of the Battle' shows such an apocalyptic war:

> Reality was given its lesson,
> Its mishmash of scripture and physics,
> With here, brains in hands, for example,
> And there, legs in a treetop.

In Hughes's modern world, with the religious instinct relinquished, we are left in a living hell with bodies and brains without souls, unstoppably driven by desire, sexual and otherwise. There is no God, no soul and no afterlife, only a slowly decaying body and a fragile brain on a journey to oblivion. It is an honest, though brutal picture.

Whilst thinking of *Crow*, I wondered whether my quest for understanding my malfunctioning brain had started much earlier than my research on the changing nature of memory in the twenty-first century. Ever since I was a small child, I have been fascinated by what to me today still seems the biggest mystery in the universe: the human experience – of *being*, of *being here*, in this world. What is its nature, how does it work, what does it mean (if anything) – and where does it go after the light goes out (when we sleep; when we die)? And what is the human mind – or consciousness – anyway? Vladimir Nabokov said: 'Consciousness is the only real thing in the world and the greatest mystery of all.'

But when did this quest start, I wondered? I knew it was to do with my religious upbringing – and my loss of faith at the age of twelve when I instinctively understood that for me the church was not able to explain how human beings and the world work. As a small boy, I grew up in a Catholic part of the predominantly Protestant Netherlands. At the services in the late seventies and early eighties, I was bored, choking on the stale-musty air, half-looking at the proceedings in front of me, but more interested in deciphering the stories depicted on the stained-glass windows. We knelt on hard, wooden planks and recited prayers. The villagers put money in a red velvet bag attached to a golden stick – for the wealthiest it was a moment to show off, carefully rustling their salmon-pink 25-guilder notes. At the end of the service, we were called forward by the priest, and waited in line. When it was your turn, you'd close your eyes, open your mouth and stick out your tongue: the priest would put the wafer, stamped with the seal of our community, in your mouth. The body of Christ felt soggy, and would stick to the roof of my mouth.

Religion was made to seem so important by my mother, by my Catholic primary and secondary schools. When my cousin was diagnosed with leukaemia at the age of three, my mother made my sister and I get on our knees to pray to make him better. Twenty years later, when we had a drink in a bar, I jokily asked him to buy me a round because he owed me: my prayers had worked.

A Trickster in My Head

The moment I realised I could not believe in religious doctrines was an epiphany, but it left a vacuum. I needed to make sense of life. I turned to art and literature – I wanted to become a film director, but after being rejected by the Dutch Film Academy, I decided – after a miserable attempt at taking over my father's company – to study English Literature. Studying stories and language was for me a particularly potent way of finding meaning in life.

As a student in the late 1990s, I remembered a shocking moment when I experienced a growing awareness of my consciousness of experience, and experience of consciousness. I was really enjoying the feeling of being in the world – aided by the smoking of cannabis (I lived in Amsterdam, after all), which I used to write song lyrics for my band. I liked the associative logic that marijuana induced, precisely what good song lyrics need. The shock came when I realised that someday there would be a world without me in it. Impossible! It was an insult to my very existence, which seemed so smooth and continuous that I couldn't imagine it would ever cease. I realised a paradox: that I could now, right at this moment, imagine a future world where I would not be present, though in that future world I would no longer be present in the world to experience it. Perhaps I would be a rapidly fading memory in a friend's mind, or Facebook would posthumously announce my by-then 112th birthday to my friends (who would also be physically dead but virtually alive), yet the brutal world, which continued spinning, would shrug its shoulders, uncaringly. My bodily matter would be reunited with the universe, my consciousness released from its obligation, or ability, to make me feel so profoundly present in this world.

At university, I took some philosophy classes and came across René Descartes, the seventeenth-century philosopher. Descartes questioned everything, including existence itself, except for the existence of the soul, and in the age of Enlightenment where better to imagine the soul's location than in the central station of reason: the brain. He also introduced me to the mind-body problem and proposed a system of dualism which argues that the physical body and the mind are completely separate from one another. This surprised me. I thought the mind was generated by the body and brain in order to regulate the collection of sensory impressions from the outside world, so as to form the subjective stream of consciousness that is our everyday experience, whereas this French guy argued that the mind was purely a mental, immaterial phenomenon that has autonomy and is divorced from the body. Living four centuries earlier in a profoundly religious, Catholic world, Descartes linked the mind to the soul, which he thought resided in a tiny organ in the brain called the pineal gland, an idea that for us seems preposterous. In ancient and medieval times, the pineal gland was thought to regulate the flow of animal spirits, an idea refuted by Galen of Pergamon two thousand years ago. The point is that the possible importance of this organ was on the radar of cultures very early on.

I also encountered artists who, in search of the soul, drew inspiration from our cranium's enigmatic content. Michelangelo had once stated that 'A man paints with his brain and not with his hands.' The Italian polymath Leonardo da Vinci was obsessed with the brain and, at the start of the sixteenth century, was seeking the seat of the man's soul in the human body. Da Vinci had access to human bodies from the Santa Maria Novella hospital in Florence, and used new techniques to capture the inside of the skull. With molten wax injections he made impressions of the cavities where the elusive soul might be hidden.

Already in 1759, Laurence Sterne's early classic novel *The Life and Opinions of Tristram Shandy* was poking fun at Descartes, who was struggling to reconcile his own quest for knowledge and 'Enlightened' concepts with religious doctrines. *Tristram Shandy* is a bawdy philosophical rumination using the stream of conscious technique – way before the modernists did at the start of the twentieth century – to explore various philosophies, including John Locke's theories about human existence.

Sterne would not tolerate Descartes' idea that the soul

inhabited the pineal gland, and in a famous passage his Uncle Toby spoils the fantasy for Shandy's gullible father:

> Now, from the best accounts he had been able to get of this matter, he was satisfied it could not be where Des Cartes had fixed it, upon the top of the pineal gland of the brain; which, as he philosophized, formed a cushion for her about the size of a marrow pea; tho' to speak the truth, as so many nerves did terminate all in that one place,— 'twas no bad conjecture;—and my father had certainly fallen with that great philosopher plumb into the centre of the mistake, had it not been for my uncle Toby, who rescued him out of it, by a story he told him of a Walloon officer at the battle of Landen, who had one part of his brain shot away by a musket-ball,—and another part of it taken out after by a French surgeon; and after all, recovered, and did his duty very well without it.

Despite my own instinctive understanding that there isn't such a thing as soul that is located in your brain or your heart, I had grown up believing that there was such a thing as a soul in the first place. I wasn't the only one. Imbibing the Catholic doctrines from the earliest age, Joyce uses the word 'soul' 202 times in a variety of meanings in *A Portrait*: the novel is, amongst other things, a meditation on the nature of the soul, especially in the chapter where he considers becoming a Jesuit priest:

> What did it avail then to have been a great emperor, a great general, a marvellous inventor, the most learned of the learned? All were as one before the judgement seat of God. He would reward the good and punish the wicked. One single instant was enough for the trial of a man's soul. One single instant after the body's death, the soul had been weighed in the balance. The particular judgement was over and the soul had passed to the abode of bliss or to the prison of purgatory or had been hurled howling into hell.

Perhaps Joyce had read about a bogus experiment. In 1907, an American physician from Massachusetts, Duncan Mac-Dougall, wanted to prove his hypothesis that souls are material. MacDougall measured the weight of six people in nursing homes whose death was imminent – as well as fifteen dogs. He wanted to prove that humans have souls and animals do not, as Descartes had claimed three centuries before him. The experiment was completely bogus, as MacDougall threw out evidence (from an already unscientifically small sample size) that didn't suit his hypothesis, and his methods made it impossible to measure the changes in weight accurately. MacDougall focused on the result of only one 'participant' who apparently lost 21.3 grams at the moment he expired. Still, the experiment made the headlines.

We have a hard time letting go of the idea of the soul. I don't believe in the soul anymore, though I miss the idea of a shared eternal and immortal essence, not because it offers the promise of an afterlife but because it provides something fixed inside of me: my character. And this is why my stroke was particularly upsetting as the emotional and physical turmoil divorced me from what I thought was me. The ensuing depression, isolation, and anxiety were character traits that I didn't associate with myself. It was, in fact, the very opposite of the 'character' that I saw in the mirror, and on my CV.

Aristotle called the soul *psyche*, a structure of rationality that is close to what we today call consciousness, a highly developed intelligence structure that processes sensations and thought). Yet I prefer Raymond Williams' concept of 'structure of feeling', a specific sensibility or spirit that belongs to a *Zeitgeist*, a political and cultural era. I like to think this structure of feeling can also be used to understand places (let's say, a house and a garden) and events (like a protest, or a music festival), but also the self: character is not simply about how a person perceives. Jane Austen calls it 'sense and sensibility', but we now usually call it a 'vibe'.

I'm not the only one missing (the idea of) the soul. There is a curious passage in Kazuo Ishiguro's novel *Never Let Me Go*, which traces the lives of a group of clones who have been created to provide organs. The novel raises concerns about the state, and status, of humans in our troubled modern world, and makes a claim for art's profoundly ethical and critical vision. Towards the end of the novel, the protagonists Kathy and Tommy have a chat with their former teacher, Miss Emily, who reveals that the clones were asked to make art for a particular purpose: 'We took away your art because we thought it would reveal your souls. Or to put it more finely, we did it to prove you had souls at all.' The idea that artistry is evidence of a soul is a humanist vision in which art and learning are able to pinpoint a certain structure or form of an organism – a character that perhaps unconsciously longs for the idea of the soul.

I suspect that Ishiguro may have read Oliver Sacks's *The Man Who Mistook His Wife for a Hat*, in which he describes the case of a man suffering from Korsakov's syndrome, whereby severe alcoholism leads to irreversible amnesia. Sacks notes the fact that the patient is aware of a loss of his sense of self because he cannot remember parts of his own life. Sacks starts to wonder if the man has been 'desouled' by his disease and asks the nurses at the hospital a startling question: 'Do you think he *has* a soul?' The equation of the soul with memory is an important hunch, though: the 'soul', the psychic dynamo behind our character, is driven to a significant degree by how we remember our thoughts and actions during our lives.

Perhaps my own obsession with understanding memory as a key component to one's personality came out of my loss of faith. Church, ironically, made me realise I was a materialist and not a spiritualist. Almost instinctively I understood that, when looking at Jesus's tortured, bleeding body hanging from the cross, it is the body and the brain that generate the mind – and subjective experience, the feeling of *being here*. My stroke was a confirmation of my theory. Yet my theorising didn't offer any consolation. There's nothing when the light goes out: consciousness switches off for a final time, the molecules of our bodily matter are ready to reunite themselves with the universe.

I realised, as I was still wandering the neighbourhood park, that I was deeply lost in my associative musings. I'd never seen my brain at work in this way, meandering and swirling like a river that had burst its banks, following the battered folds of my brain.

When I returned home from my GP visit, a letter had been delivered, and it yanked me back to reality. The envelope had '**Private and Confidential**' printed on it. Exciting. MI5 was finally offering me a job, I thought.

It turned out to be a letter from my university discussing the return-to-work protocol. The words were written by my Human Resources Adviser, whose usual matter-of-fact tone was now leavened by a compassionate note: 'I can't find the right words to properly empathise with you', it stated. (Neither can I, I thought.) But my bosses had a genuine concern for me, which was a great relief. My university was treating me like a human being. My Head of Department wrote: 'Dr Groes is a reliable, innovative and valued member of this university's academic staff.' She continued:

> Our concerns are for Dr Groes' recovery and optimising his chances to do so; at the present time our concerns are that Dr Groes may return too early and/or take on too much to facilitate an optimum recovery. Any advice in relation to a phased return, techniques to support a successful recovery, regularity of breaks, etc. would be very helpful.

Seeing this in black on white made it real again: the stroke, my affliction. There were consequences. I needed to see a consultant at the Occupational Health Department at Kingston Hospital, south-west London, where a consultant would assess the state of my health and provide advice on my recovery and any adjustments that needed to be made. I was also invited to make use of the university's Employment Assistance Programme, which offered advice on a wide range of 'life events', a euphemism for a wide variety of human problems, including illness, stress, depression, harassment, bullying, divorce, self-harm and suicidal tendencies.

In a discussion with my line manager, we talked about the psychological implications of my stroke for my work but also far more existential matters: the fact that I had come close to death, that I was lucky to be alive. 'Yes,' I joked during a post-stroke meeting with her, 'one moment you're immortal and invincible and a good night's sleep later you're a mortal.' I agreed it was a good idea to see a shrink to talk about the brain meltdown and its psychological implications. My close encounter with death, the loss of a sense of immortality that comes with youth, how to deal with unexpected emotions such as loneliness and depression. And, of course, how my aphasia would impact on my performance.

Before the stroke, confidentiality didn't mean much to me. I'm a Dutch guy and had lived life in a relatively unguarded way. It was a cliché, but in the Netherlands, the living-room curtains are always open – nothing to hide. The world of the Dutch is transparent, open: there isn't anywhere to hide in the flat, completely artificial landscape. The Dutch lifestyle is quite a bit different from the English way of life, with its intricate behavioural and cultural codes and subtle, circumventive use of language – people's keeping themselves to themselves and their station, preferably behind closed doors with the curtains drawn. But now I felt exposed and vulnerable – I wanted to draw the blinds, yet it was too late. My stroke had scraped away a protective layer of what I thought of as my character. The armour of my ego, which admittedly wasn't in short supply, had been penetrated. I felt naked. The world was looking right into the ruins of my life.

Chapter Seven
The Brain, Within its Groove

In those post-stroke days, the first thing I did every morning when I woke up was to say *portomonee* out loud a couple of times, a litmus test to check whether I hadn't had another infarct. The word had become a shibboleth – a password that reassured me I hadn't had another stroke.

Back then I walked through a small, hilly forest that connects Crouch End with Highgate, called Queen's Wood. Climbing the leafy paths, I mumbled sentences to myself in Dutch and English. I was reciting Shakespeare's Sonnet 127 ('In the old age black was not counted fair') and Wordsworth's sonnet 'Composed upon Westminster Bridge' and some lines by Carol Ann Duffy and Liz Berry. Nothing wrong with my memory. But I did feel as if the words were spoken by someone else, and that this other person, the squatter, spoke with pebbles in his mouth. Words dropped heavily from me, bouncing off the ground with tiny ticks.

Emily Dickinson wrote a poem, famous amongst critics exploring the brain in culture, that captured my experience:

> The Brain, within its Groove
> Runs evenly—and true—
> But let a Splinter swerve—
> 'Twere easier for You—

The Brain, Within its Groove

To put a Current back—
When Floods have slit the Hills—
And scooped a Turnpike for Themselves—
And trodden out the Mills—

I experienced the gap between myself and other people as hostile disconnection, perfectly captured by Dickinson's dashes: a gap, a breach, a break. The silence implied by dashes – my broken-down, interrupted speech. Neurolinguists had measured the effects of stroke on the human voice of people with post-stroke depression: 'Impairment of affective prosody, defined as extraverbal information indicating the emotional state of the speaker, independent parameters: the fundamental frequency of the voice of the sound emission, the shimmer (small variations in glottal pulse amplitude), voice breaks, and the speech rate.' Prosody has to do with the loudness, pitch, rhythm and tempo of the human voice – intonation and vocal stress. Patients with post-stroke depression (PSD) speak louder and at a slower rate and, concerning 'reading tasks, the analyses showed that baseline voice break percentages were significantly higher in patients with PSD'. My impaired ability to communicate was evidence of the break within myself, the collision between my former and post-stroke self, a mismatch between my perception of the world, and the world's actual attitude to me.

Even though I wanted to pretend everything was alright, and that nothing had happened, I noticed that I wasn't myself. There was a war raging inside my head. The clot was a minuscule mortar attack with explosive consequences. There was a conflict between my former ego, the personality that I wanted to return to, and the victim of a neuronal attack who was trying to survive.

I was aware that I was using conceptual metaphors to grapple with my situation. I'd noticed this first during the stroke event itself, when I was using the radio image to understand the stroke's impact on my consciousness and the headlight image to explain alterations to my perception. As I couldn't put what was happening into words, I used symbols to describe what I was going through. I was using these images to capture a very complex experience. I was aware that the war analogy was a specifically masculine metaphor. The comparison was violent, and perhaps grotesque and a bit stupid?

The changes to my personality were undeniable. I'd lost confidence in my former self: the more I'd try to act like him, the more I was confronted with the fact that I simply no longer could. It was very confusing. I felt lost.

And I was also 'agitated'. I wanted to get back to work, but to do so I needed to go for a check-up and interview as part of my Occupational Health assessment at Kingston Hospital. So I took buses, the tube and a train to southwest London.

At the hospital, in the uncomfortable heat of the Indian summer that had descended on the city, I couldn't find 'Occupational Health' on any visitor information signs. The hospital was a brightly coloured maze that confused my navigational skills, and no one I managed to stop knew where this department was. I traversed the wandering maze of A&E, tried the cancer unit, visited Blood Tests and circled my way back to reception, none the wiser. After a phone call, I walked to the back of the medical campus to find a yellowed sheet of A4 paper – with 'Occupational Therapy' scribbled on it – taped to a dusty window. I was sweating, my shirt stuck to my back and my brain pounded in my skull.

I hoped the consultant wouldn't be failing me for my sweaty, dishevelled appearance. She was a professional. I sensed coolness. Her verdict had much weight: she could force me to stop working for three months or perhaps even a year. The advice this independent medical judge would give was legally binding for my university. I felt authority bear down on me tangibly. I didn't want to lose the life that I had built up for over a decade, nor the future I'd planned for myself.

After taking a deep breath, I told the consultant that I was doing well. This was not a lie, depending on how you looked at the situation – I was alive, after all. If I could convince her that I was doing alright, then surely my chances of continuing to work would increase? My blood pressure satisfied her, which surprised me after the ordeal I'd just gone through.

This was the only physiological test she did. I told her I would undergo a series of tests led by a neurologist at the Royal Free Hospital, and that we had to await those results. She asked whether my cognitive and motor functions had been impaired. 'Nope,' I stated firmly. What were my daily challenges? I wanted say, 'If I'm honest, avoiding people's brain waves, steering clear of noise, shielding myself.' But I didn't.

I didn't lie to her, not really. I was just underplaying the effects of the stroke because I did not want to admit that anything was seriously wrong. I sported a face that combined seriousness with a tentatively optimistic smile, a KEEP CALM AND CARRY ON attitude, which my GP would have approved of. I wanted to keep leading my memory project and feared that taking a full autumn term off, as colleagues and friends had suggested, would result in intellectual paralysis and reputational damage.

The problem with the questions I was getting was that there was only one verifiable source who was answering them: me. So I did have some power in this process, but I was, stupidly, using it against myself. I told the consultant that I was sleeping a lot, and that I was taking things easy and that I had some trouble writing, but that it was already going much, much better. I suggested that I continue to take it easy, doing only three hours of teaching per week, that I work with the neurologist and that I visit a psychologist, and that we should expect that I could return to work fully in the new year. My speech hardly carried a trace of the attack, now. I let the words roll off my tongue, hoping she would agree to it.

She did. In front of her sat a man, still youngish (if thirty-nine is youngish) who, despite having suffered a stroke, seemed full of energy. This man wanted to get on with life. Why not let him?

Mission accomplished. I made a deal with the consultant to take it easy for the next three months and after that return to work 100 percent. Result! After I got back from the hospital, I collapsed in my bed for a two-hour nap.

I noticed other changes to my daily life. Automatically I kept on touching the place on the left side of my skull below which lay deceased brain cells. I found the idea that inside my brain there is a graveyard of organic matter disconcerting. Weirdly, even before seeing the MRI images on the day after my stroke, I was able to sense the place where my brain had been ravaged by the blood clot. I sat there, my hand on my skull, the warmth of my fingers sinking into the thin skin that covered the bone. A friend of mine, Jason Tougaw, wrote about the fantasy 'whereby touching brains may reveal the stuff of which self is made'. There is always, as Jason explains, an explanatory gap: the brain is not the mind, nor the self. I know this. Even so, I already sensed that there was a great intimacy about calling this cerebral event *my* stroke: something so troublingly private and unique. I was trying to touch my brain to comfort it, to heal it.

Another thing I noticed: I wanted to live a healthier life than I had before. I needed to take care of myself and cook well, so I made a Gado-gado, a cold Indonesian meal consisting of steamed cauliflower, French beans, potato, cucumber and bean sprouts, accompanied by peanut sauce. José was half-Indonesian, and I was addicted to the Indonesian cuisine she and her family had introduced me to. Normally I'd have a beer, but now I drank a glass of water alongside it.

Maybe it was because I was doing everything much slower, more consciously, but my taste and smell were definitely more acute. The starchiness of the rice was more pronounced, and I thought I could taste the ginger and cumin on my taste buds. I did some research in my enhanced ability to taste and smell and found out that this was a *sensory disturbance* – a post-stroke disability.

I started investigating my condition in a more structured manner, like a good scientist. I analysed how my speech and writing continued to be affected. My speech was still partly disabled but seemed to be doing much better: I still spoke slower than I used to, but I could articulate my thoughts relatively well. I looked back at some of the crippled emails in the direct aftermath of the event, and then started typing a few new ones. I also tried to write a paragraph of academic prose, but the sentences derailed, still. I subdivided my glitches into categories:

(1) It takes me longer to think of multisyllabic words. I sometimes start to write sentences, and at first my fingers follow my thought, but after a few words my brain suddenly can't keep up or cannot help find the right words, especially longer ones.

The voice inside my head, the ticker tape called consciousness like the news crawler at the bottom of news channels, had been running slower, certainly in the first few days after the stroke. Now, when I needed to come up with three- or four-syllabic words, I often 'felt' them, but I couldn't produce the goods. They were on the tip of the tongue, but it took me ten to twenty seconds to come up with them – if they came at all. Words like:

combobulation
sophistication
indefatigable
extemporaneous
predisposition
quintessential
conciliatory
penultimate
deferential
cumbersome
sanitisation
instantaneous
commensurate
denominational
tangential

They were hard words, now, but words I used to have no problem with. I knew I knew them, that they had definitely been deposited in the stuff inside my skull a long time ago, but at the moment I felt I needed a crowbar to prise them free.

(2) It takes me longer to think of words that are not part of the world's Standard English vocabulary or of Euro-

English. I have also lost my feeling for slang that belongs specifically to local English or American cultures.

Things like: 'ebullient', 'cauterise', 'prim', he has a 'dowdy' look, 'tatty', she has a 'frumpish' appearance, 'valetudinarian', 'don't fret', 'ta very much', he's such a 'prig' (a Danish translator friend's favourite word), the heat made the tarmac 'shimmer', I feel 'frazzled', we went on a 'recce' (according to my cosmopolitan London friends), he has a 'fractious' character, a 'tacit' understanding, the 'incumbent' president, the cats were 'caterwauling' all night, excuse the 'tardiness' of my response, 'tattie', 'I've broken me leg and they're taking me down the 'ozzy'' (Liverpudlian for 'hospital' – I'd lived in Liverpool for three years), and a 'chip butty'. I noticed myself thinking less of such words. In fact, I felt a pang of shame when I heard such words pronounced or when I saw them written down, in novels or newspapers. I was afraid that I'd lost a part of my vocabulary, but also that I'd lost my sense of embeddedness in English cultural localities.

(3) Spelling is difficult; sometimes I don't see that I'm actually writing the wrong word, like I'm dyslexic.

Do you 'poor' or 'pour' a drink? Was I 'exited' or 'excited'? If you are 'exited', someone kicks you out. Were you 'exstatic' or 'ecstatic'? Was it 'practise' or 'practice'? Did you prove your 'metal' or 'mettle'? I always spelt the verb 'harness' wrong anyway – with a second 'a', because I associate it with the Dutch word *harnas*, which means the same thing.

This was all a bit embarasing. Or embarrassing. One of those two. But also a huge problem: if I lost my ability to spell, how was I going to write articles and books and correct student essays? How much extra time would this cost me, and how long would it take before these disabilities faded?

(4) I mix up English words that look alike, but have a different meaning.

I noticed that I messed up the distinctions between 'their', 'they're' and 'there', for instance, and I really had to think about which words I was supposed to be using. I also had problems with 'your' and 'you're'. I saw that I had accidentally substituted 'thought', 'through' and 'taught' as well. It was slightly difficult being a writer who no longer knew how to distinguish a preposition from a possessive.

(5) My English is affected much more than my Dutch.

I wasn't a native English speaker and it seemed that my English language skills had been eroded. Over the past decade, English had become my first language, though. The ticker tape inside my head spat out English most of the time. I dreamt in English, even if it involved scenes set in Holland or Dutch people. My Dutch had become colonised by English, and often I inserted English words when I spoke Dutch, for convenience's sake. I also produced transliterations from English to Dutch. This linguistic transformation took place because of my immersion in English literature and because my circle of friends consisted mainly of English people and Americans.

Now, however, my writing showed that my native language base had survived the stroke better than my adopted linguistic skills. My Dutch acted differently from my English; it was not embedded more deeply within my brain, but just in a different area. I was experiencing *selective aphasia*. But I also learned a hopeful fact: bilingual skills enhance stroke recovery. 'The percentage of patients with intact cognitive functions post-stroke was more than twice as high in bilinguals than in monolinguals', a study noted. And apparently bilingualism leads to a better cognitive outcome after stroke, possibly by enhancing cognitive reserve. 'We'll see about that,' I said to myself.

By making this list I felt I was controlling these disturbances a little. What struck me, though, was the disjunction between the way my speech and writing were able to convey my thoughts. Usually there was a good match between how my voice verbalised my thoughts and how my hands wrote or typed them. But now a gap had opened up. My hands betrayed the working of my mind – another disturbing mismatch.

Yet there were other positive developments. I was reading memoirs by fellow stroke survivors, including Robert McCrum's *My Year Off*, Jill Bolte Taylor's *My Stroke of Luck*, and Maria Ross's *Rebooting my Brain*. Although I didn't know them personally, I felt close to these writers: our brain trauma united us. They too made lists to regain control over their lives. McCrum made lists of the major themes of his life, of Dos and Don'ts for the convalescent stroke sufferer, for instance. Bolte Taylor had a list of forty things she required most after her stroke, but mostly the need to find 'deep inner peace', which she found in gardening. I was a gardener too and was also drawn towards tending my vegetable patches.

It seemed that all their stories had a similar outcome: a new perspective on life, on selfhood, and a re-appreciation of love and friendship. In all of them, a reprioritisation took place, and warmer, more empathetic people had emerged. In her conclusion, Ross talked about the fact that she no longer had to be a superwoman, and admitted that people should acknowledge that they are more vulnerable that they think; after her stroke, she looked at life differently. McCrum noted: 'I have learned […] that I am not immortal (the fantasy of youth) and yet, strangely, in the process I have renewed my understanding of family and, finally, of the only thing that really matters: love.' Stroke survivors were all (even more) grateful to their loved ones, and were full of love. I was a bit surprised by the endings of these books. I didn't feel (and couldn't imagine) catharsis at all – I was a depressed, confused mess.

My perplexity took me back to the moment of the diagnosis, which should have brought clarity, but didn't. When the neurologist delivered his verdict ('two strokes', which turned out to be a misdiagnosis, it was 'just' one brain attack), two contradictory things happened. I was stunned, nailed to the floor, speechless still, not because of the stroke but because my body had become a seismograph registering a devastating existential earthquake. Yet part of me instinctively wanted to breathe a sigh of relief, and say, 'Ah, of course, that makes sense.' At the same time, I resisted the French-inflected words that came fluently from his mouth. I happily accepted this judgement, this fact, and refused to believe it, as I knew it to be false at the same time: curious Orwellian Doublethink.

In hindsight, my condition was obvious, but in the midst of the event it was far from clear: confusion, terror, paralysis – a speechlessness that literalized my inability to explain what had been going on inside my head. Even though this revelation may be uncomfortable, the clarity it provides yields great comfort. The neurologist's explanation was like *anagnorisis*, as Aristotle calls the key moment of discovery in his definition of Tragedy in *Poetics*. *Anagnorisis* and *diagnosis* are judgements, moments of understanding and insight. Both reveal the 'true' identity, or nature, of people: you can turn out to be a psychotic incestuous killer, as is the case of Oedipus, or, for instance, suffer from autism spectrum disorder, which may explain social-interaction difficulties and communication challenges. And understanding how a situation has arisen gives us a euphoric moment of bliss – an epiphany.

This intuition wasn't too far off. The cognitive neuroscientist John Kounios notes that the right hemisphere plays a key role in creative insight, as it makes connections between things that don't seem to fit together well. He says that, before a moment of insight, it is first the back of the brain, home to the visual cortex, which is active: this part helps solve puzzles in an analytical fashion, and it looks to the outside world for information to make sense of. But then a change happens: the left hemisphere (responsible for processing language and concepts) is turned on, though there is less activity taking place. Kounios states: 'This is the mind turning in on itself. This is the mind disengaging from the world. This empowers a person to imagine new and different ways to transform reality creatively into something better.' Kounios calls this 'inner directed thought'; he also cites the Post-Impressionist painter Paul Gauguin, who said: 'In order to see I close my eyes.'

So, once again the modernists were there first. This epiphanic 'inward turn' was already apprehended by James Joyce in the 'bird girl episode' in *A Portrait of The Artist as a Young Man*, to which I adverted in Chapter Two above. Joyce's epiphany follows the same pattern as Kounios' explanation: first, Dedalus looks to interpret information from the external world, whereby our senses pick up signals from the outside. After that, an inward turn takes place whereby the mind processes information imaginatively, making connections between bits and pieces of information that normally would not cohere. At that moment, insight 'arrives' – not from the outside, but from connections made within the brain.

It was illuminating to see that Joyce explicitly turns the girl he is observing into a bird. This wasn't simply a young man's objectification of an attractive young woman. Dedalus notes that there is an analogy between the pleasure we find in understanding structures in the natural world and in artistry. Joyce's epiphany fuses the two worlds of nature and art. These worlds were no longer analogous to each other, but they were welded together to become the same, inseparable and reborn. The excitement and pleasure they yield are the same. That was his discovery.

But I needed to stop this digression. There were problems with the parallel between art and life. Aristotle's literary criticism was of fiction, not of lived reality. Tragedies are dark but fictional representations that arrange life in ordered, artificial patterns; it is *tekhnê*, artifice, craftmanship. Storytelling is a medium that deploys artificial strategies to manipulate the viewer's emotions: via plotting and use of language we are tricked into feeling sympathy for a person who is wholly imagined. *Anagnorisis* and *diagnosis* are different: the former is about art, the latter about life, about 'reality' – whatever that is in a world shaped by fictions of so many kinds.

Because I was floundering, bewildered, I was reaching out to the stuff I know best – stories. But, as a professor of literature who spent a lot of his time engaging with fictional characters living lives in imaginary worlds, even though the doctor's verdict felt unreal, like a plot twist that didn't belong to my life – this was undeniably real. I had to accept I was no longer in control of the story of my life as I had imagined it to be.

Chapter Eight
Maps of the Mind

Autumn was setting in. London was rainswept and storms raged through the city's streets. I usually loved this season – a period of transformation, of stormy change. But this time, my mood seemed to be disproportionately affected by the darkening world outside. I was on an overground train to the Royal Free Hospital, just south of Hampstead Heath, watching raindrops make tracks across the carriage window. It had taken the NHS a month to make an appointment for me with a neurologist. I was carrying *Portraits of My Brain* and other medical documents. The wait for the appointment had been agonising. As soon as possible I wanted this doctor to reassure me, tell me it was under control, and the stroke was a one-off event, that I was going to recover and that all would be well. I felt let down, left to my own devices.

I had promised myself to walk at least five kilometres a day. Walking had a renewed importance to me now – a 30-minute walk every day drastically decreases your chance of stroke. My love affair with walking – walking London – started when I did my doctoral research, which investigated how writers recreated London in literature, and I started to tramp the capital obsessively. I walked the Walthamstow Marshes and broke into the Reservoirs; I had breakfast on the Beckton Alps, offering the best view of London; I re-enacted walks from novels. I built up a detailed map of London in my mind, as well as a strong mental compass, which I knew to be very important for my recovery. Your ability to plot different routes to specific geographical goals stems the effects of the ageing of the brain.

My ability to navigate London came in handy when my transfer to another overground line at Gospel Oak station was thwarted. Signal failure. No more trains. I stood on Gordon House Road, and turned left. I was sure that the hospital was to be found in that direction. I saw a letter bus, the C11 to Brent Cross Shopping Centre, whoosh by on the wet tarmac, sending water swishing. I had walked the wrong way: my inner compass was scrambled. What an embarrassment. I realised the irony that, in an age in which digital technology tracked your every move and could tell you where to go with utmost precision, I was lost. I turned around, late already, and jumped on a bus in order not to miss my appointment. Had my navigational skills been impaired? The stroke hadn't hit my hippocampi, the two small organs in the brain which help you calculate and steer through space effectively.

Recent research in mild stroke patients suggested that almost a third of them experience navigational problems and that this impairment remains quite long after they have physically recovered from their stroke. With the increase in the quality of medical care, many more patients recovered from a stroke, at least to some degree. As people's life spans were increasing, so was the total number of stroke patients. The psychological, social and cultural consequences of stroke deserved more attention.

Ineke van der Ham, a neuropsychologist with whom I collaborated, was doing research on GPS assistance as a tool for treating navigation impairment, and had mentioned an example of a patient with damage to his hippocampus. A man founded and ran a business but one day couldn't remember where he'd parked his car in the morning. His smartphone was a great help, though. All day long he made notes to remember where he had left his bike or car. He also used the route planner app when driving his car or riding his bike.

Around six months after brain damage, most patients are

stable. At this point any impairment is not expected to change without intervention. With neuropsychological rehabilitation therapies, patients can still improve substantially at this point. Modern technology, including GPS, can really make a difference:

> The most common and sensible approach is to train people in using specific strategies that will help them to compensate for functions they have lost. For instance, a patient with particular problems in using traditional maps and creating a 'mental map' of an environment will most likely benefit most from relying on the intact skill of using information provided by landmarks they encounter in the environment.

So, maybe I should use my phone more, to help me rebuild my map of London inside my brain? Or maybe this is the opposite of a good idea; perhaps technology makes the brain lazy?

> For healthy individuals, the effects should be considered from a different perspective. Studies point out that the use of GPS can make a person 'mindless' of their environment. They no longer create 'mental maps' of environments if they only interact with them while relying on GPS. Such mental maps are crucial to navigate space successfully and efficiently, as we use them for many aspects of navigation, such as determining where we are and where our goal location is, and assessing distances and efficient routes between these locations.

Perhaps I should not use my maps app on my phone, then: rely on the sun, follow my divining rod, sense ley-lines and earth rays, avoid zones of disturbance. I walked, head down, staring at the pavement, shielding myself from the rain, earphones plugged in. I felt I was closing in upon myself, and that I was losing myself. Out of character.

Finally, I made it to the neurology ward at the Royal Free

Hospital, which had a dull aura: dank, grubby light, nebulous. The neurologist let me into his office, an examination room with a desk on which stood a laptop. He was young and slim, wearing a shirt without a tie. He didn't make eye contact, but asked for the report drawn up by his French counterpart, and took me through the MRI maps of my brain, explaining the contents in layman's terms. He showed me the route that the blood clot had taken, how my heart had sent it up through the carotid artery in my neck and then firing it into the left hemisphere of my brain. The neurologist's face showed no emotion. He was impossible to read. I spied a slight excitement in his eyes when he matched the diagnosis with the images. Behind his rational façade and curative gaze, surely there was a human being who experienced emotions, hated his boss, and shed an imaginary tear when remembering the death of his first pet?

The neurologist told me that we were replacing the aspirin I was taking with the anticoagulant Clopidogrel, which works very well with the cholesterol-lowering Atorvastatin. These 'statins' lower LDL cholesterol levels by 20 to 60%, reducing vascular problems, that is to say, the clogging up of the veins with fatty lipids. Clopidogrel, the anticoagulant, has a narrow therapeutic window meaning that 'the range of the dosage [...] that is effective without producing any side effect is very narrow'. A blood test called 'international normalised ratio' (INR) is used to measure the effect of the blood-thinning. Whereas normal people will have an INR of 1.0, the goal for an ex-stroker lies between 2.0 and 3.0. Anything below 2.0 sees a waning of the effect with the risk of clots, but above 3.0 you risk the blood becoming so thin that bleeding becomes a problem. I asked how long I had to take these pills. My neurologist said that patients on anticoagulants require close and lifelong monitoring. Alarm bells were ringing.

He explained to me, fingertips touching, what 'we' were going to do. We were going to investigate my blood and my heart, and hopefully we'd find the cause, the stroke's aetiology. No guarantees, of course. We'd be looking at genetic blood diseases that could cause my blood to clot, or any arrhythmia, whereby my heart slowed down or stopped for just a moment, which could also cause my blood to congeal. *A tiny dirty bullet*, I imagined.

The neurologist took my blood pressure – 148/92 – there was room for improvement. I asked him if the worrying information about young stroke victims I found on the internet was true: the reduced life expectancy for ex-strokists, the higher likelihood of a second killer stroke? Secretly I hoped this was just an unfortunate aberration in neuroscientific research that had accidentally drifted to the top of the search engine lists. For the first time, he looked at me directly. 'Yes, all this is true. Young people who have suffered a stroke have an increased likelihood of such an event happening again. Life expectancy is detrimentally affected as well.' I felt beads of sweat on the nape of my neck. He should have said something comforting: that it was just statistics, that I could prevent early death by living healthily. 'Take it easy, and you can sneak your way into the 66%,' he should say. But he said nothing of the sort.

I surmised that this neurologist should work on his empathy skills. Patients do not want their neurologists to burst into tears when bringing bad news, but the image of the neurosurgeon as a stoic, über-rational, superhuman doctor-God was a myth. In Henry Marsh's memoir *Do No Harm* the neurosurgeon admits: 'The idea that neurosurgery is some kind of calm and rational application of science […] is such utter crap. At least it is for me. That bloody operation last week made me feel as nervous as I was thirty years ago.'

'Do you have any other questions?' the neurologist asked. Like my GP, he too was in a hurry. My head was buzzing, but I was trying to collect myself. I told him that I was disproportionately anxious and angry, and sometimes I seemed to have no emotions at all. I was usually collected, cool, courteous, but now I was short and snappy with colleagues, wanted my friends to leave as soon as they arrived, disliked speaking with my family. 'Yes,' the brain whisperer stated, 'it's not unusual for your behaviour, your emotions to change. It may take a while before things settle down again.

I'd give it a year.'

A year?!

There was another, more practical question. I told him that I was about to turn 40 and that I had planned to play a reunion gig with my band: 'I'm the singer.'

I detected a frown on his unreadable face. 'No, I think I'd advise you against that. It would be best to avoid any strenuous activity for the foreseeable future.'

Damn. 'What about physical exercise?' I asked.

'You can do some running and go to the gym, but no heavy weights lifting or any exercise that puts a lot of pressure on the brain. Just take it easy. Do you understand the gravity of what happened?'

And what about flying? 'I would advise you against long-haul flights for at least three months. And when you do, get an aisle seat, so you can walk around regularly. You want to avoid thrombosis.' The doctor handed me a slip of paper that showed a raft of blood tests I needed to do. The NHS would be in touch once they had the results. It could take a while.

I had the samples taken straight away. The nurse was impressed by the list of investigations. 'Are you sure you want to do this in one go?' She collected what felt like five buckets of blood, taped cotton wool onto my arm, and I was on my way.

Outside, the north London air tasted like an electrical current, iron-like, as if I had put a nine-volt battery in my mouth. I needed a different route back to the train station, and took a fork leading left. As I was walking, a voice in my head said: *You're gonna die, sucker.*

What struck me was that this neurologist offered me only prohibitions – don'ts. He was clear on what I shouldn't do, but not on what I should do to take care of my body, my brain and my mind, which was not doing too well. Neither he nor my GP warned me of post-stroke depression, and how to handle it. Walking, a healthy diet to keep my blood pressure down, for instance, I had to Google to find out. Research showed that aquatic exercise lowers the levels of depression and anxiety in people who have suffered an ischaemic stroke.

Other light exercise has similar effects, and singing in particular has marked effects on post-stroke recovery.

Why was no one mentioning this to me? No one talked about the impact of stroke on, for instance, sexuality. People who had suffered strokes sometimes saw a major change in their sexual lives: some had a decreased interest in sex due to fatigue or a decreased sensibility. Others experienced a positive change in sexuality because they feel closer to their partner and experience an enhanced need for intimacy. We needed to talk about such issues; the medical profession should not be prudish. We could be grown-ups about matters that are central to our lives. But it seemed to be a no-go area for doctors. A study by neuroscientists states that '[v]ery few informants had received any information or discussed sexuality with health care professionals during the six years after the stroke, although such needs were identified by most informants'. Instead, they suggested that when it comes to sexuality, the medical professional left many needs unmet. Maybe it's just a specifically English issue, I wondered.

Deeply immersed in thought, I lost my way again. I needed to ask a passer-by for directions, and she pointed me to the C11 bus. This loss of my navigational skills was troubling me just as much as the loss of my language. 'London is a language,' as the novelist David Mitchell once said. But it seemed to be a tongue I no longer spoke. What was I to do?

On the bus, I remembered Iain Sinclair's novel *Radon Daughters*, which mentions a character who projects the X-ray image of his cancer onto a map of London and starts to walk the city obsessively to cure himself. Perhaps I should project the MRI-image of my wounded brain onto London, and hike it back to health: the walking cure.

The science fiction writer Adam Roberts told me that Charles Dickens – another obsessive London psychogeographer – also used walking as a cure for disease. In the late 1850s, Dickens suffered from insomnia and went on nocturnal ramblings, leading to *Night Walks*, an exploration of the down-and-outs in Victorian London. Throughout his writing life, he exhausted his body unrelentingly. Dickens wrote an extraordinary amount every day, went on shattering theatre tours in the UK and abroad, and was an obsessive walker of London. This exhausting lifestyle had a detrimental effect on his health, which was already declining. Although he was able to disguise his physical frailty, around 1868 he suffered a big stroke, or perhaps a series of minor attacks. Dickens was also misdiagnosed: although early interpretations of his symptoms pointed to frostbite and apoplexy, a critic has suggested that the right parietal or parietal-temporal lobe of his brain had been affected. This diminished the left half of his normal vision: for instance, he could not read the left side of shop signs. Dickens' friend Watson noted:

> He had some odd feeling of insecurity about his left leg, as if there was something unnatural about his heel; but he could lift, and did not drag, his leg. Also he spoke of some strangeness of his left hand and arm; missed the spot on which he wished to lay that hand, unless he carefully looked at it; felt an unreadiness to lift his hands towards his head, especially his left hand – when for instance, he was brushing his hair.

The (mini-)strokes continued. In a letter to John Forster written on 22 April 1869, Dickens observed a curious incident that had happened to him: 'At Chester last Sunday I found myself extremely giddy, and extremely uncertain of my sense of touch, both in my left leg and the left hand and arms.' He had taken some light medicine and wondered if the meds had caused this loss of sensation, but his doctor assured him it was his overworked body (and brain, presumably). He continued:

> The left foot has given me very little trouble, yet it is remarkable that *it is the left foot too*; and I told Henry Thompson [...] that I had an inward conviction that whatever it was, it was not gout. I also told Beard, a year after the Staplehurst [train] accident, that I was certain that my heart had been fluttered, and wanted a little helping. This stethoscope confirmed; and considering the

immense exertion I am undergoing, and the constant jarring of express trains, the case seems to me quite intelligible. Don't say anything in the Gad's direction about me being a little out of sorts.

Dickens wasn't just a little out of sorts: he had suffered a minor stroke – and more were to follow. His 'inward conviction' was correct: his brain was spluttering due to his deteriorating physical condition. At the age of 58, on 9 June 1870, Dickens died of a stroke.

London, brains, walking, writing, navigation. Once again, I scanned *Portraits of My Brain Just After the Attack* and looked at the photos of my wounded head. What came to my mind was an image called *Hippocampus* that Kathy Prendergast made for *The Cabbies' Shelter Project*, an art project raising awareness about the historical role that the green, wooden shacks for taxi drivers had had in London life since the late nineteenth century. Prendergast conceived of London as an organism, a brain:

> I wanted to concentrate on the idea of the city as organism, the cabbies as ferrymen and the cab shelters as locations of navigation expertise. To trace the 320 routes of The Knowledge along the streets and roads of London is also to trace the information that enlarges the hippocampus. My idea was to see what this would look like. Was there a visual equivalent between the maps of London and the cabbies' brains? Is this information a reflection of the inside or the outside, microcosm or macrocosm?

Prendergast made this drawing in translucent ink showing the road system of London: the routes, the junctions, the roundabouts, the bridges, an analogy for synapses, the Willis Circle, the hippocampus, etc. She explored 'the possibility that they could be the same thing'. She was not far off. In 1978, the Nobel Prize-winning neuroscientist John O'Keefe published his ground-breaking study, *The Hippocampus as*

Cognitive Map, which shows that the hippocampus generates 'place cells' when we visit a location, and our brain remembers this place. There is a correlation between the external world that we journey and an internal map that is created by our brain.

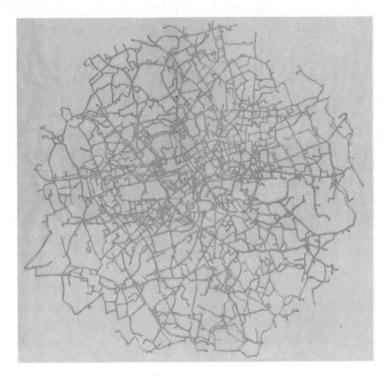

Figure 5

Prendergast's image was fascinating, beautiful, and I could imagine that a blood clot, in the form of a car crash, would block an artery, a road, an area, a postcode. What was I supposed to do? Walk London to break up the clog and restart circulation? I was no longer sure I believed in the classic, organic metaphors that would recuperate a sense of my humanity now that my glitching brain was disconnecting me from the world. I was aware that the brain and physical space were not the same thing, though I knew there was a link.

I was far from clear what it was, exactly. During that immediate post-stroke period, I didn't feel that metaphors or beautifully sculpted language would heal me; I needed something real, something tangible – literature seemed to be merely a Band Aid that would not help me with what I was really in need of: not a poet, but a neurosurgeon that would fix my brain and ensure that this calamity would never happen again.

What was happening to my belief in words? The more I clawed at the history of literature, the less I felt it could heal me, or even offer comfort. The voices that had spoken to me from the fiction that had determined my life for over twenty years were barely audible. Perhaps the shock of the brain attack was too undeniably real. My history of London walking had layed down maps in my brain, and my reading had given me imaginary worlds that had left traces in my grey matter – fictional maps interwoven with my real journeys in physical space.

But it was not enough. I felt alone (but not lonely) and I deliberately abandoned my friends and family, and it seemed I was losing faith in fiction. I needed something real, something tangible, but the overwhelming sense of loss, of feeling lost, was disconnecting me from myself. My ambitions had crippled my personal life and connection with my inner self. And now, even my own brain had told me to bugger off.

Chapter Nine
A Concise History of Stroke

It had been thirty-three days since I had been struck down by a brain infarct. I was learning a lot about what had happened to me. 'Struck down' is a phrase that derives from the same etymology as 'stroke'. Yet, I'd come to learn that 'brain attack' was the popular term that scientists and doctors preferred over 'stroke', as this term conveys the actual nature of a brain infarct – a serious medical emergency involving the brain. 'Stroke' was too simplistic, capturing what the phenomenon looks like from the outside – someone being clobbered on the head. But with the development of medical science, especially in the post-war period, and the increasingly detailed knowledge about the nature of neuro-infarcts, the wide variety of conditions associated with being 'struck down' was better conveyed by 'brain attack' – as in 'heart attack', also a phrase that acts as an umbrella term for many different types of heart failure or issues.

My normal life was kicking back in, at least to some degree. Today I found myself standing in front of eighteen eager students who were taking *Poetics of Surveillance*, a course that investigated surveillance via literature, from the Bible and Dickens' *Our Mutual Friend* to Jenni Fagan's *The Panopticon*. I arrived early to re-arrange tables and chairs whilst running through my introductory lecture, mentally editing, adding and deleting the words and phrases of a twenty-minute talk. I was self-conscious, nervous. The surveillance students were unaware that a small part of my brain starved to death a month ago. Teaching that the omnipresent eye of God which always observed you created a 'split self' because you inevitably internalise His viewpoint was not helping to keep my character together.

Speaking in front of audiences did not come naturally to me: I used to be cripplingly shy and stutter and stammer when thrown into the limelight, red-faced, sweating. During my first job as a lecturer, I forced myself to memorise fifty-minute-long lectures. I mastered my rhetorical performances in front of the mirror. Slowly I became alright, then good, then quite persuasive. I learned that the persona belonging to my public, professional life was to a large extent a performance, a confidence game.

The students entered the classroom. A new academic year was starting, full of potential and new challenges. They strategically distributed themselves across the seminar room, some talking excitedly, some silent, eyes locked on the screens of their mobile phones: some last-minute texting, posting.

I spoke. 'Welcome, everyone…' The voice in my head and the one that actually resonated in the class room didn't quite match up. There was a gap between how I thought I would sound, and the voice that emerged from my mouth. It was like hearing a recording of myself on a tape recorder, which always feels as if it is not you who is speaking. This auditory dissonance distracted me, and I felt my mind splitting – both delivering the lecture whilst pondering why the hell my voice sounded different. Surely the students had noticed this? Did they realise my brain had been hacked?

Paranoia kicked in and my ability to find the right words slowed down. Words like: 'carceral', 'fuselage', 'overzealous', 'dissymmetry', 'manifestation' and 'mandate'. To me there seemed to be eternities of silence between the words I was pronouncing. The 'errrrrrrr'-ing whilst I scanned my brain. Maybe they would think I was a bit rusty after the summer break. Instinctively I reached with my hand for the left side of my head, touching the part of the skull where, just a few centimetres below the surface, things weren't right. To the students this gesture must have looked like I was thinking really hard.

They didn't realise, I learned later. On the feedback forms my students were nothing but complimentary, praising the intellectual challenges the course presented them with. A year later a student was shocked when I revealed I was teaching whilst I should probably have been taking time off to recover. 'I hadn't noticed,' he said. 'There was nothing to notice, as far as I can remember.' I was relieved. What did it say about the perception of twenty-year-old students who didn't see that in front of them was a guy whose speech was letting him down? Or had I been able to cover up my linguistic fallibilities through sheer experience? Or maybe I was just exaggerating it all? I wasn't sure of my capacity to judge the situation correctly.

During the seminar break, I went for a coffee. A colleague approached me and expressed her worry about me, and told me that the department was concerned, but also relieved that, well, you know... 'Yes,' I filled in her three dots. 'That I'm still alive.' I felt tired from the class and my colleague talking so very quickly that I only managed to say, 'Thank you. It's been difficult, but I think it's going to be alright. I just need time to recover.' I realised that my colleagues were burdened by my stroke: they had been asked to take on extra teaching and marking. I was ashamed about this, and wondered if I should apologise. Instead, I fled the scene. I wasn't sure how to deal with people, especially those with overdeveloped linguistic capabilities.

The weekend I spent by myself, alone, reading a bit and trying to repress the urge to work. I wandered about the garden a little, tidied up a bit, but my lust for gardening had left me. I Skyped with my parents. I told them how I was doing, but I was feeling really uncommunicative. I was irrationally irritated by my mother's questions. She insisted that she was coming over from Holland the next weekend to help me out. She felt sorry for my being alone. I told her I didn't care about my predicament, which wasn't really true. I just wanted to be alone, to be left alone.

To get a handle on my situation, I did more research into the history of the brain and neuronal crashes. A concise history of strokes and the treatment thereof started, as far as I could tell, with 'trepanation', the practice of drilling holes in, or cutting or scraping away the bone of, the skull. Trepanation took place as long ago as 5,000 BCE. Scientists were not entirely agreed on why this custom took place: some evidence suggests that Neolithic populations drilled, cut and scraped to cure headaches, skull trauma and brain diseases. Releasing pressure on the brain by drilling holes that allowed excess blood to escape is an operation that, in the case of haemorrhagic strokes, is still used today. Thousands of trepanned skulls had been found on archaeological sites across the world, but the need for crude surgery also had another, perhaps primary, ritual association: trepanation was part of initiation rites, but also used to release (evil) spirits from the body – or to allow the passage of good spirits to the inside.

A cultural critic stated that 'such interventions in the shamanistic faith are used to recover the lost soul and the medical reasons cited later on are only rationalizations of these mythical arguments'. Recently, anthropologists had found in several places in southern Russia skulls of various individuals dating to the Neolithic or Bronze Ages (somewhere between 5,000-3,000 BCE) that had been trepanned in an unusual manner, suggesting a ritual and not a medical procedure because no evidence for trauma or pathology was found in the skulls. Others speculated that these trepanations 'may have been performed to achieve "transformations" of some kind'. One researcher suggests that 'by trepanning [...] people thought they could acquire unique skills that ordinary members of society did not have'. So, 7,000 years ago, our ancestors were (possibly) engaged in experimental, unnecessary brain surgery to see if they could change and extend people's normally limited abilities. We don't really know, but the idea that people will always try to create better versions of themselves fascinated me.

With some exceptions, this crude practice, which was also

used to try to cure epilepsy and 'melancholy' (depression), had stopped by the end of the Middle Ages. One of the most famous medieval allusions to trepanation was Hieronymus Bosch's *Extracting the Stone of Madness*, painted about 1494. The painting shows how a 'surgeon' wearing a foppish overturned funnel for a hat, and with a wine bottle dangling from his belt, is cutting open the skull of an elderly man (Lubbert Das) to excise his supposed madness – which in fact is foolishness. The madness has taken the metaphorical shape of a tulip (in a Dutch proverb a 'tulip head' referred to a simpleton). Next to the doctor and patient are a monk who is chatting to the quack and an uninterested woman who doesn't seem to be able to understand what to do with a book, which she wears like a hat. The stonecutter was not a figure from reality but existed in the late medieval period in parlance only; the imagined figure exploited the stupidity of the equally fictional Lubbert Das. Bosch's humorous, ironical image shows that the supposedly learned, sane doctor is far less rational than the patient he is trying to cure, and his brain surgery shows the worst excesses of an insanity that is clearly apparent to all except himself. The painting served as a warning against deceit and foolishness, and promoted the need for scepticism towards the promises of quacks.

What we today call neuroscience started to really develop from about 1,500 BCE, evidenced by the Egyptians' Ebers Papyrus. This twenty-metre-long scroll consisting of 100 pages was among the most important ancient Egyptian *papyri* (a medium for writing, made from the papyrus plant) that set down hundreds of folk remedies and magical formulae, but also contained medical procedures and practices. The scribe provided advice on contraception and mental health issues, including depression. He also had a remedy to stop 'too frequent evacuations' (diarrhoea): take fresh *dart* (the pulp of a quint-apple), fresh porridge, oil, honey, wax, and water; boil this concoction and eat for four days. The manuscript also evidences a quite sophisticated idea of the brain's anatomy, aided by the fact that the brains of mummies were extracted through the nose.

Even so, it was the heart that was still central to thinking about the human body. The heart connected all parts and organs with one another: 'There are vessels from it to every limb. As to this, when any physician, any surgeon or any exorcist applies the hands or his fingers to the head, to the back of the head, to the hands, to the place of the stomach, to the arms or to the feet, then he examines the heart, because all the limbs possess its vessels, that is: the heart speaks out of the vessels of every limb.'

Around 460 BCE, the Greek physician Hippocrates argued that all disease was caused by an imbalance in the four humours or temperaments (blood, phlegm, black bile and yellow bile). He stated that the brain was associated with intelligence and sensations, the heart with the passions. The Greeks had an influential idea about the mind, which they called *psyche*. The Stoics believed that the *psyche* was the 'soul' of people, and that this soul resided partly in the heart. In the fourth century BCE, the philosopher Socrates broke free from the idea of the brain-dominated body and relocated the seat of intelligence and feelings in the heart. For Socrates, the heart was the most important organ of the body and the brain was just a phlegm-producing system that cooled down the heart. Socrates' student Plato also believed that humans possessed a soul, and he divided the *psyche* up into three parts: rational thoughts, the passions and desire. It was people's duty to train the logical part of the *psyche* to curb the forces of appetite, located in the lower belly. The 'life-soul', the passions and desire, were situated in the heart. The only immortal part of the soul – our essence – was located in the head. This fallacious opposition between the heart and the brain as metaphors for a clear-cut distinction between the passions and rationality has remained intact in the popular consciousness ever since. This unhelpful contrast between subjective and objective approaches to medicine that I experienced after my stroke can be traced back to Greek doctors working two thousands year before me.

Yet major strides in thinking about medicine and the brain continued to be made. Around 280 BCE, Erasistratus studied the brain and distinguished between the cerebrum and cerebellum, and he described its divisions. A while later, the Greek physician Galen of Pergamon (129-216 AD) offered the first theory that the human mind was generated by the brain and not the heart. He dissected animals and described some of the major veins in the brain. In 171 AD, Galen gave an important lecture on the brain. Much of his research into the brain's role in generating the mind persisted for over 1,500 years.

The Greeks and Romans knew almost nothing about brain infarcts, though from the historical record we know they occurred. The closest they came was to diagnose strokes as apoplexy, a bleeding of the internal organs. Etymologically, the word apoplexy is close to the word stroke, though: it literally means to be 'struck down' or 'a striking away'. It was only in 1658 that Swiss physician Johann Jakob Wepfer came up with the theory that ruptured blood vessels were causing apoplexy in the brain. We now know that this is the case in about only 20 percent of stroke sufferers (the bleeders); four out of five strokes are caused by a blood clot getting stuck in a blood vessel in the brain (the clotters).

Only since the seventeenth century have physicians and anatomists slowly started to publish on the brain's anatomy. Rather than drilling holes, the practice of bloodletting was a popular response to the disease associated with stroke; bloodletting, it was thought, reduces blood pressure – an idea that was discredited only in 1935. From the 1970s, stroke databases aided researchers and doctors in understanding brain attacks. American President George Bush declared the 1990s the Decade of the Brain because modern technology created the opportunity for increasingly complex research.

So, for millennia, the heart absorbed much attention from scientists, even up until the late twentieth century; research into the brain and treatment of brain disease – aided by new technologies – has only started to flourish in the past decades. Neuroscience is a young discipline, a toddler amongst the sciences. Its new understandings are timely. As we now live longer, we are all on average more likely to suffer a stroke.

Modern lifestyles also increase our chance of suffering strokes: obesity and high blood pressure are two risk factors that increase the chance of brain attacks.

My research into neuroscience was helping me get a hold on my situation – or, at least, the rational ordering of knowledge allowed me to imagine I was able to exert some kind of control over my predicament. But there was another way in which I was trying to heal myself. In the immediate aftermath of my stroke, I tended to go more often to classical concerts, mostly by myself, on a few occasions with a friend. I remember a Sunday night, a month after my stroke, when I went to the Barbican, where pianist Nicolai Lugansky performed Britten, Prokofiev and Shostakovich. As usual classical music had an effect on me like Ritalin, the drug that helps ADHD sufferers concentrate: any chaos in my life would become ordered. I left the auditorium with a neatly arranged To-Do list.

When I listened to most classical music pieces I felt cleansed and my life was restored to order. When I listened, for instance, to the finale of Mahler's *Resurrection Symphony*, the choir at the end of the piece had a cathartic effect on me. Work by modernist composers such as Debussy, Ravel, Shostakovich and Stravinsky set my brain alight, as neuroscientists would say. In *Musicophilia*, a book about people with a deviant experience of music, Oliver Sacks gives a clue to the effects of classical music on the brain: 'Music has more ability to activate more parts of the brain than any other stimulus. Music seems to be a cultural invention which makes use of part of the brain developed for other purposes, not only auditory parts, but visual parts, emotional parts, and, at a lower level, in the cerebellum, all the basic parts for coordination.'

This connection between the brain and classical music wasn't new. I'd read *Self Comes to Mind*, a book by neuroscientist Antonio Damasio, in which he sought to understand how primitive parts of the brain were involved in the creation of one's character. Damasio compares consciousness to the execution of a symphony of Mahlerian proportions. But the marvel [...] is that the score and conductor become reality only as life unfolds. [...] The grand symphonic piece that is consciousness encompasses the foundational contributions to the brain stem, forever hitched to the body, and the wider-than-the-sky imagery created in the cooperation of the cerebral cortex and subcortical structures, all harmoniously stitched together, in ceaseless forward motion, interruptible only by sleep, anesthesia, brain dysfunction, or death.

Susannah Cahalan's *Brain on Fire*, an autobiographical account of how a rare auto-immune disease attacked her brain, resulting in paranoid hallucinations and, ultimately, catatonia, also compared the brain to an orchestra:

The healthy brain is a symphony of 100 billion neurons, the actions of each individual brain cell harmonizing into a whole that enables thoughts, movements, memories, or even just a sneeze. But it takes only one dissonant instrument to mar the cohesion of a symphony. When neurons begin to play nonstop, out of tune, and all at once because of a disease, trauma, tumor, lack of sleep, or even alcohol withdrawal, the cacophonous result can be a seizure.

Damasio and Cahalan use this comparison between an orchestra and the brain (and self) in a metaphorical way. They are trying to translate how consciousness works by means of a strong, pertinent image. But, as Sacks suggests, there isn't merely a metaphorical connection between the two. Neuroscientific research has demonstrated the strong emotional effects of music on the brain. Listening to Stravinsky's *The Rite of Spring* or reading Kant's *Critique of Judgement* – both pretty 'difficult' experiences – had extraordinary effects on the brain, research had shown. In the film *Alive Inside*, patients lost in oblivion due to Alzheimer's disease were momentarily brought back from life-in-death when they listened to music from their youth and teens. The point was not that music can revive brain cells – in the case of Alzheimer's, parts of the brain have atrophied – but that the music triggered other parts of the brain, and thus contributed to bringing back (happy) memories and changing someone's overall mood for a period of time. This helped restore a sense of self – and some kind of humanity – for patients and their families.

I sensed that the effect of classical music also reconnected me to my former self – a younger and livelier person, a guy that now lived only in my memory. I was reminded of Murakami's *Norwegian Wood*, in which music triggers memories of Watanabe's youth – and set the story in motion. When he lands at Hamburg airport, a muzak-version of The Beatles' song 'Norwegian Wood' starts to play from the aeroplane's ceiling speakers. The song, from the *Rubber Soul* album, kickstarts an immediate physical response – a musical or auditory version of the Proust Phenomenon.

Watanabe's quest to preserve and understand the past and his former persona resonated with me. At home, I caught myself picking up my acoustic guitar and strumming its rusty strings. I played some classic songs from when I was beginning to learn the guitar: 'House of the Rising Sun', 'Hotel California', 'Redemption Song', 'That Boy', 'Polly' by Nirvana. I was going back to the start, to my nineteen-year-old self. I tried a few jazz chords that my father-in-law, who had died in 2005, taught me a long time ago. I was getting back into the groove. My fingertips hurt. I was out of practice, but I liked the feeling of becoming one with the instrument – humming along with the tunes.

Perhaps this increase in my visits to classical concerts and return to playing my acoustic guitar could be explained because I felt, almost instinctively, that music contributed to healing my brain. But there was another reason as well, to do with my aphasia. My language had been affected, and language is a figurative medium. That is, language is made up of words, and words have a specific meaning and point to concrete things in the world – 'cat' refers to a domesticated animal, and 'Westminster Bridge' evokes an architectural structure. Perhaps I turned to music because it is more abstract, less directly associated with the world, with which I was losing my connection because my ability to name and describe it had become weakened. Something similar happened to the twentieth-century Belgian-American writer May Sarton. Unable to write after her stroke, at first she was unable to listen to music at all 'because it had been so closely connected with poetry', but soon she regained a sense of the importance of the non-figurative: 'this is a trip to the border of wonder world – where words lose their currency, and symbols speak by themselves, as Music would'.

The effect of a stroke on Dickens suggested a similar move. Towards the end of his life, he continued with his performances, even though paralysis was setting in. He continued work on his final novel, *Edwin Drood*, which he left unfinished as he died of a massive stroke after a full day working on it. His writing itself had become affected by the strokes as well: in the note that contained a new chapter for the novel the writing is so cramped, interlined and blotted as to be nearly illegible, according to Dickens' biographer John Forster. The series of small strokes Dickens suffered during the final year of his life resulted, perhaps, in the dominance of music, musical notes and tones in the novel. Jasper, *Drood*'s villain, is a composer of church music, and the trick with the murder is that the murderer is able, in the pitch dark, to find the appropriate key in the bunch of keys by striking it against stone and discerning its tone. I wondered if a potential obliquity of words in Dickens' mind moved his imagination in a musical direction. Dickens' aphasia possibly forced him, perhaps unconsciously, to reach out for a non-figurative art form.

I was coping with my brain attack, which had disconnected the wires in my head, by fusing back together knowledge about neuroscience, art and literature. Walking, music, I tried them all. I hoped that, by connecting science with the history of culture, I would be rerouting the brain activities that had been disrupted, that brain cells could be re-connected in a new way. I understood that I was changing in the process, and I could feel this transformation in the core of my very being. To move forward, and work through my head trauma, and accept that a different personality was emerging, it was important to address my past self as well. It was probably a smart idea, as my Head of Department had noted, to get professional help with my psychological metamorphosis.

Chapter Ten
Emotional Dyscontrol

My black-out sleep continued for weeks after the stroke event until I experienced a dream so vivid it was indistinguishable from waking life – unexpected, pure. The dream began with a voice transporting me back to when I fell in love for the first time. I was in the middle of nowhere, in a barn built alongside a railway track; the walls' dark oak panelling was lit up by flickering candlelight. '*Hoi Bas*,' a girl's voice said to me. 'What's happened to you? You look worried.' I immediately recognised the voice as belonging to my first girlfriend, Maaike. I stared at the pale Ophelia face exactly as it was when I was fifteen. My fingertips glided around her eyebrows, nose, lips, her chin. She took my hand and guided me into a hall with people sitting around tables, drinking, some wearily lost in thought. Hushed chatter. Electric lighting, pulsating. These dark figures, hunched over the tables, faces half covered in shadow – a waiting room in a strange train station from Victorian times.

'It is so good to see you again,' I said. 'I can't believe how long it's been. I thought you were…'

Maaike shrugged her shoulders. 'I couldn't stand it anymore.' She smiled and said nothing for a bit. The honey-yellowish flicker of flames made everything glow. She said, 'You have stuff to take care off, things to work out. It was good to see you.' She placed a kiss on the left corner of my mouth,

113

just like she used to.

The image of the waiting room crumbled and disappeared, she was gone and I woke up, gasping. I didn't want to leave the dream world, because for a moment it allowed me to postpone confronting the fact that my first love committed suicide two months before the stroke. I hadn't heard her voice for so long, yet it was so deeply familiar. She was locked inside my skull, had nestled herself in my grey matter during my teens and, so I had just discovered, never left.

The news of her death had come as a great shock. I hadn't heard her voice for so long yet it was deeply familiar. This wasn't memory, it was invention: my brain was imaginatively reassembling and extrapolating bits and pieces of memory – experience – laid down twenty-five years ago. I was sending messages to myself. My first love died, and I half-died, within the space of two months: my unconscious was linking these two events and was trying to make sense of the deaths of these two lovers. Part of my brain was trying to put both events in a logical, causal relationship, even though they were completely random. All the time the brain twists experiences to make sense of them, edit and re-order them so that they are accommodated in a smooth story that underpins the idea we have of ourselves and how we fit into the world.

Our love was no common secondary school love. The intensity of our relationship scared our parents. Not us: we knew our love was right and true, infinite and forever. It was, perhaps, unhealthily overpowering, not that different from Romeo and Juliet – an obsession, a pathology. We didn't break up: we were broken up. Her mother forced us to terminate our relationship, not only because she thought I was not worthy of her only daughter – to her it seemed to stand in the way of the natural development of our personalities. It had to happen; we knew that. But the hurt was so bad I swore I'd never fall in love again.

Our love was an important experience for me, illustrating that unconditional commitment can very easily be trashed by the ways of the world. But the experience had not proven transformative enough for me, and this is what I wanted – to change. I wanted to transcend my background, my origins, and acquire an artistic sensibility. I had no doubt I belonged in Hollywood, writing and directing movies. I grew my hair, bought army boots and a woollen black- and red-checked lumberjack shirt like Seattle grungers had. A girl, hair shorn, pale, not like Ophelia but more like a committed drug addict, asked if I could sing. I said I'd try, and before I knew it, I was on stage performing indie rock. Within weeks my transformation was complete.

My first love's unhappiness would prove fatal twenty years later. Struggling with her weight and self-esteem for nearly four decades, and diagnosed with a bipolar disorder too late, she stepped in front of a train, ten miles from the place where we grew up. Destroying her body was the only way to escape the torture of her existence.

Even though we'd lost touch twenty years previously, the knowledge that she existed somewhere, living her life – walking, eating, chatting and sleeping – had been comforting. It was soothing because she was the only one who could corroborate the past reality of our relationship, our joint story. Now, she is no longer in this world. It's as if I'm the last remaining speaker of a language, a particular way of thinking and being is gone.

The hallucinatory vividness of the dream could be explained because of brain plasticity. The cortical reorganisation meant that old electrical circuits that have been damaged are rerouted via other areas of the brain left undamaged: I suspected it had re-activated parts that are connected to my teenage memories now brought back in a lifelike dream.

Daniel Dennett pointed out the power of dreams in a thought experiment: he asked you to *imagine* someone kicking your shin with a steel-toed boot. Although we may feel pain when *imagining* being kicked in the shin, *dreaming* being kicked in the shin feels much more real – we seem to be experiencing pain (almost) just as much as in reality, though the pain in the dream does not have an actual physical origin.

But the intensity of my own dream suggested to me that I was undergoing a combination of brain repair with the unconscious processing of traumatic news. It was another kind of Proust Phenomenon, the reviving of memories from one's early life.

The next day, haunted by the oneiric encounter, I tried to write a few emails, but my spelling was still malfunctioning. I wrote 'speeching' instead of 'speaking'. 'Hospital' was now 'hispotal'. My hands didn't know the difference between 'its' and 'it's'. I worked on a new book and wrote 'why the modern reader should be suspician against realistic literature'. Suspician? I could have sworn my fingers were typing 'suspicious', like my brain ordered them to. I was getting even more frustrated, and angry and scared.

My quest to understand my stroke needed to continue and I made some headway with my post-stroke rehabilitation. On a website for neurological disorders and stroke I'd found out that there are five types of disability associated with stroke, some physical, some mental, some combined:

1. paralysis or problems controlling bodily movement;
2. sensory disturbances and pain;
3. problems using or understanding language;
4. problems with thinking and memory;
5. emotional disturbances.

I seemed to fall into a fair number of these categories. Although my motor functions were fine and I had no droopy mouth, my speech and ability to write were impacted by my stroke. My memory was intact and my thinking was perfectly fine except that I was just very tired. My emotional life was more pronounced, bewildering. Devoting my life to scholarship for nearly twenty years had made me good at playing the detached, hyper-rational academic, but now my emotions lay much closer to the surface.

Even though I had been confronted with the word by the French neurologist and by both the The Glasgow Outcome Score and The Modified Rankin Scale, I realised that I was disabled. The very idea struck me as so alien, so not me. I felt ashamed at the thought of not belonging to 'normal people' – but I immediately understood that I needed to correct my reaction. The moment brought me an insight into how prejudice works, how biases are all around us. My reaction came from an *ableist* point of view: for me able-bodied people are at the centre of the world. The point was that the very fact that I didn't see myself as disabled and that I was shocked to realise that I was showed how many of us unconsciously discriminate against disabled people. My horrified reaction to the idea that I was disabled showed my own blind spot but also suggested that people desperately want to be considered 'normal' – that having a disability is somehow wrong and that we need to cure this disability so we can (re)join the pack of normal people. I knew that Disability Studies had theorised all this over the past decades but experiencing it first-hand was still a shock.

I also knew that I should now consider myself as 'neurodiverse', the idea that all human brains vary when it comes to learning, attention span, mental functions and capacity more broadly. Some brains, as in the case of people with autism, produce different forms of sociability and mood. Advocates of neurodiversity argued that simply saying that people with autism or ADHD are disabled or not 'normal' is fallacious because we should conceive of the brain's abilities in a more complex manner. We are all different, neurologically speaking, though there are many 'neurotypical' people. The neurodiversity movement argued that we should not want to treat neurodiverse people for being different, to 'make them better', but that society should itself change to accommodate people who are more impacted by their brain's state.

A stroke is different from autism and other natural neurological differences because it is non-innate; therefore, the person who might have had a comparatively similar brain to most people may suddenly find that their changed cognitive abilities force them to accept that they are different, not just from their former selves, but from the cosy club of 'normal people' that they thought they used to belong to. We are all different, all 'other' – though we should surely be careful to understand the needs that severely disabled people have. The power of the 'difference' point of view was shown by an experiment with neurodiverse students, including one who had suffered a stroke. These students were divided up into two groups: the 'difference' group in which 'neurodiversity was seen as a difference incorporating a set of strengths and weaknesses [and a group with] a "medical/deficit" view – where neurodiversity was seen as a disadvantageous medical condition'. The results were stark: 'The former view was associated with expressions of greater career ambition and academic self-esteem, while the latter view was associated more with processes for obtaining the Disabled Students' Allowance.' In short, the difference point of view leads to an empowerment position that has a subtle understanding of the pros and cons of your position, whilst the 'medical/deficit' view leads to a disempowering, victim-like understanding of one's situation.

This research and theory were helpful to me, and these debates felt even more urgent because I could see directly – painfully personally – how they related to my own experience. I needed to accept that I was disabled, perhaps temporarily, but it was clear that the experience was leaving its traces in me. The attack changed my outlook on myself.

To help me with the many questions and uncertainties that were troubling me, I was to see a psychologist. The NHS asked whether I wanted a man or a woman as my psychologist. I said I'd prefer a woman. When José and I were receiving counselling for infertility trauma, we worked with two women psychologists. I wasn't the blokey kind. So, the NHS allocated me a man. Women are in higher demand in this profession, I was told.

My shrink's office was in Highgate, a couple of miles to the east of my home. I walked through Queen's Woods, a medieval forest whose leaves had now turned yellow and auburn. It was early October, and in the back of my mind was my birthday – my fortieth.

In the reception area, the secretary was busy on the phone, so I sat down. The woman wasn't looking at me and did not acknowledge my presence. When she was done, I walked up to the counter to give her my name. She continued to avoid my eyes, making me feel insecure and a little ashamed. This was a demonstration of the so-called 'theory of mind' – people's ability to imagine what other humans are thinking. I thought that this secretary was avoiding eye-contact because she pitied me. 'Look at this poor thing, physically robust, but his mind shot to pieces. An emotional wreck. No good anymore. Garbage.' I was projecting imaginary thoughts onto this person, who was simply incredibly busy and was respecting my privacy. I was over-interpreting the situation completely. A red-eyed patient left the counselling room without a word. 'A fellow loser,' I thought, 'also unable to handle the pressures of modern life.' I was getting even more nervous. My mounting insecurities were exacerbating my paranoia.

My shrink let me into his room. We sat opposite each other in lazy chairs. Behind him was a small clock, staring me down. We engaged in some chit-chat. My psychologist turned out to be a guitar player, like me – a nice, but totally coincidental connection. He struck me as a pleasant fellow, probably married with a couple of kids, living in a posh bit of north London. Not old money but privileged enough. At a barbecue, he'd be someone you could have a conversation with about the latest Tate Modern exhibition or current politics and the most recent popular science books. He knew his wine and was a self-declared foodie, but he'd attempt to hide the accent that betrayed his upper-middle-class origins. And I, a down-to-earth Dutch classless guy, was supposed to be opening up to this type?

'How are you doing?' he asked me. A simple question, with complex answers. I said I felt vulnerable, exposed – and depressed: 22.5% of people with a stroke suffer post-stroke depression, and I was one of them. The normal conception of myself and the world had derailed. I was emotional and afraid of the future. Most of all, I was weirded-out by the fact that I seemed to need to say farewell to my pre-stroke personality, and that I had experienced a memory trigger in the French hospital that brought back my younger, youthful self, a sensitive, vulnerable boy. 'Is it possible that the ghost of a former version of yourself can haunt you? I asked.

I spoke about the unexpectedness of the event. 'I didn't see this one coming, because it happened on the inside. You always expect violence to come from the outside: a car crash, a punch in the face, a fall down the stairs.' It had been such a surprise, an unforeseeable twist at the end of a movie – it lay beyond the realm of possibility.

I told him the stroke event itself reminded me of Kafka's story 'The Metamorphosis', in which Gregor Samsa wakes up to find he's turned into a bug overnight. Into vermin. He lay in his bed, on his back, small useless legs waving about, unable to do anything. But his mind was still intact, and trying to make sense of what the hell had just happened. That's how I woke up, a month ago – physically powerless, my body turned into that of a lesser creature, but my perception of my identity still whole. At least at first. But ever since, my personality had been changing, unravelling – the knot that held the jumble of my former identity had become untied. I felt trapped, imprisoned.

I used to love Kafka's story about transformation, I said to my shrink. Fifteen years ago, I even adapted it into a song, I loved the idea so much. But now... now I was living the story. And I now truly understood what the story is about. Just like poor old Gregor, I could feel a conservative pull inside, a search for safety by fleeing towards my family, to my wife, and embracing my role as an academic just as Gregor wanted to return to his office where he worked as a clerk – the exact reason he'd transformed into a low-life in the first place. And the loneliness. I'm not sure if it's loneliness, exactly, maybe it's more a desire to be alone – aloneness. Whereas I was outgoing and had a huge social life, I now enjoyed solitude. I didn't mind the gap that had opened up between me and the world. Strangely, a sort of uncaringness, a disinterestedness sat inside me – and weirdly was quite comforting.

The psychologist nodded and told me this was normal for people recovering from brain trauma. It was usual to experience a transformation of sorts. Sometimes it would be temporary but sometimes the changes to the patient's personality were permanent. I might find it difficult to accept such changes to my personality, he told me, but I also needed to understand that, even though he could help manage the process, many of the changes I could do nothing about.

We can talk about your metamorphosis, though, he said. It's a cliché, but lives run their course like rivers. Most events and psychic transformations do nothing but reinforce the permanence of your identity – of your character. But there are some events that have such an impact that the river splits and is diverted from its natural course and a new, unprecedented persona comes to life, which becomes the new version of you. The disruption is so severe that a radical new identity emerges. A form born of the accident, born by accident, a kind of accident. A funny breed. A monster whose apparition cannot be explained as any genetic anomaly. A new kind of being comes into the world for a second time, out of a deep cut that opens in a biography.

I told him that I wasn't sure that a radical *new* me was emerging out of the stroke's attack on myself. Yes, the changes, the disruptions to the flow of my personality had felt violent. But it seemed that what was emerging was more a marriage of my younger self and the person I'd grown into over the years. A fusion, a new balance, perhaps?

To understand that younger self, he suggested that in the first session we create a rudimentary mindmap of what kind of guy I am – or was, highlighting formative and difficult episodes in my life. 'How long have you got, doctor?' I asked him.

I ran through the major events in my life, and at various points the shrink said, 'That must have been difficult.' He was also asking me, 'How did that feel?' Some memories, such as my parents' first divorce when I was five, were enveloped in a thick mist. But even José and our disastrous infertility journey, much more recent, was something my brain did not seem to want to access: the memories were stored in a mental shelter with ten-foot-thick concrete walls.

Whilst prodding around in stories and emotions I'd sealed away, I realised it felt very good, it's a form of confession – a release. An unburdening.

Tears made tracks down my face. My psychologist handed me tissues. I wasn't crying necessarily because of talking about emotional episodes in my life. It was the stroke, and the imbalance it had caused. My body needed to cry, it seemed; I didn't have any power over it. But it was such a relief, I embraced it fully. This was *emotional dyscontrol*, my psychologist noted, one sign of post-stroke emotional disturbances caused by alteration in my brain networks. Neuroscientists called this *affective modification*, which means your emotions are all over the place after a stroke. It could lead to depression, anxieties, and even psychosis. This happens particularly when your left hemisphere is hit, as mine had been, my shrink told me. The right hemisphere of the brain is involved more fully in states of fear and anxiety, and the left is associated with states of joy and relaxation. Patients who suffer a stroke in the right frontal area show an increased dominance of the left hemisphere, and they often report a lighter mood following recovery. But if your left area suffers a stroke, the right hemisphere, which is known to influence emotional communication, becomes more dominant in shaping your mood: patients feel more worried and tense than they did before their stroke.

Dyscontrol was a scientific term for chaos. This emotional anarchy worried me. I didn't want to let go of the cool self that I'd carefully constructed, and which I could perform so well. 'But how can I know what a genuine emotion is, then?' I asked my shrink.

'You can't,' he retorted. 'It's just hormones and chemicals hitting the brain in certain spots.'

'That's genuinely messed up,' I concluded.

Prometheus came to my mind: the Greeks thought that emotions were housed in the liver, just as the Enlightenment champion Descartes thought the soul sat in the pineal gland.

The myth of Prometheus had set up an early tension between feelings and rationality: this trickster – another trickster! – stole fire from the Gods and gave it to us, humans. He came to embody the quest for scientific knowledge. He was punished for this crime with eternal torture: chained to a rock, an eagle would eat his liver, which would grow back at night, a depiction of which I'd once seen in the Musée des Beaux-Arts in Brussels. Prometheus' torture was a metaphor for the eternal struggle between the head and the heart. The ancients and Descartes were both wrong: there is no discrete separation of emotion and reason. It is wishful thinking that blinds us to the fact that we cannot separate the rational being from our feelings. Yes, emotions are partly regulated by the brain. But the brain's operations are also determined by emotions, as neuroscientist Joseph LeDoux's *The Emotional Brain* examines in detail. LeDoux views 'emotions as biological functions of the nervous system'. He argues that 'figuring out how emotions are represented in the brain can help us understand them'. He rejects the more typical approach of studying emotions as psychological states, 'independent of the underlying brain mechanisms'.

I found LeDoux's position a bit radical; the provocations of a neuromaniac. His was a narrow view. I did believe that we have a *psyche*, a consciousness that gives us a certain autonomy – maybe not much, but we have some power over who we are and how we behave. At that moment, I couldn't help the fact that that my body needed to cry, but trained actors were able to conjure up emotions – and tears. If we believed that the brain determines everything we (can) do, this meant that we didn't have responsibility for our actions. This led to a moral vacuum. There must be a psychological self that was aware of itself and controlled our thoughts and actions, at least to an extent.

Mary Shelley was already aware of this. Her novel *Frankenstein*, whose subtitle is *Prometheus Unbound*, is a story in which the scientist Victor Frankenstein's manic quest to become godlike by taking over creation leads to a similar Promethean form of insanity. She portrayed the scientist as an ambivalent figure whose quest for enlightenment led to an all-consuming obsession, madness, and the deaths of those around him.

'This tussle between feelings and reason, and the complex war between desire and angst for transformation, I know them all too well,' I said to my head doctor. The hour had drifted by in a dense haze of words and tears.

My psychologist looked at the clock. 'Time's up. Bas, you need to give yourself a break. You have suffered a major brain injury. Take it easy. Don't be so hard on yourself.' I told him I appreciated his advice, but, as I threw my tear-soaked tissue into his rubbish bin, I couldn't promise him that.

Chapter Eleven
Shits and *Goddamnits*

Everything was settling, kind of. The session at the psychologist gave me a sense of relief, and control – a perspective on myself. A new routine, the slowness of which was bothering me, had emerged, but it was a pattern, nonetheless. I slept long hours, fed myself, and did a bit of work, though the previously skewed work-life balance had tilted in favour of my personal life. My mind unencumbered by the pressures of work, I was reading, walking, cooking, going to the South Bank for classical concerts and to the Garage for gigs. The four events on memory I was organising for the Cheltenham Literary Festival were coming along nicely.

Teaching continued, I went to the gym to do some light exercise – no running, just the cross trainer and some cycling, no weights. I couldn't be bothered to travel up to work much, since I only had to be in one day to teach. I didn't see the point of sitting behind my desk in my office whilst I could stay in the comfort of my home doing the same work without losing two hours travelling. In my diary I spotted a departmental meeting, but this bureaucratic grind was the last thing I needed. I decided to skip it.

This was very uncollegial of me, and I felt guilty but I was focusing on myself, working on my recovery. The world seemed to drift ever further away. I read news headlines but I did not care much about what was going on. The world seemed less important, now. All my hard work had been for nothing. I might as well be dead, I was thinking dramatically. I thought about alternative professions if my aphasia persisted, but I wasn't sure what. Farmer? Tax inspector? Taxi driver? Being a writer would make me happy, but that goal was very hard to achieve now as I still wrote sentences that derailed:

> *Today I went to the doctor to pick up medacition an chekc my bloed presure but I do not stil feel rihgt in the hed*

It took me a long time to get it right. It was deeply frustrating. I wanted to hurl books across the room.

But once more literature proved useful in helping me understand my predicament. I was looking for more fellow stroke survivors. The writer May Sarton left an extraordinary body of work behind: a total of fifty-three books, including nineteen novels, seventeen books of poetry, fifteen non-fiction works, two children's books, a play, and additional screenplays. Nowadays she was hardly read by the public, though she still enjoyed a strong reputation amongst writers – Sarton was a writer's writer.

Born in Belgium, the young Sarton moved via England to the States, though she spent a formative period in the 1930s in Paris, where she met Virginia Woolf and Elizabeth Bowen, amongst others. Her first novel, *The Secret Hound*, was published in this literary *milieu*. Almost fifty years later, the prolific Sarton suffered a brain infarct, the recovery from which she described in *After the Stroke*. The first paragraph captured exactly her bewildering post-stroke experience:

> It may prove impossible because my head feels so queer and the smallest effort, mental or physical, exhausts, but I feel so deprived of my *self* being unable to write, cut off since early January from all that I mean about my life, that I think I must try to write a few lines every day.

The estrangement, the exhaustion, and the loss of selfhood were all too familiar to me, as was the frustration about not being able to write properly. She noted: 'I have no surface energy because reserve energy has to be built back first.' And: 'I lie around most of the afternoon, am in bed by eight, and there I lie in my bed alone the past rises like a tide, over and over, to swamp me with memories I cannot handle. I am fragile and naked as a newborn babe.' She was angry and weepy because 'simple things seem impossible', and her sense of smell had markedly improved: 'The most tasteless foods now acquire loveliness: an oatmeal becomes a poem of fragrances. An egg delivers exquisite life to my sick brain.' I hear you, May, I thought.

What struck me also was that, like Dickens, Sarton's uncompromising attitude to life and literature had taken its toll:

> I am too vulnerable to all the losses and often the pain connected with personal relationships. I have had too many lives, have attached myself to so many people over the fifty years since I was twenty-five [...] during those fifty years I have lived hard and to the limits of my capacity as a human being and as a writer. So it is a huge bundle of feelings and thoughts that ride on those tides when I lie awake at night.

Sarton's use of the word 'bundle' was striking: it seemed to suggest that she saw herself as a multiplicity of persons with 'many lives' squeezed into one lifetime that had been characterised by pain and loss that now, at this moment of post-neurological crisis, confronted her with questions about, and challenges to, selfhood and identity.

Sarton was aware that her identity, her self, had come about through her interactions with many different people who had shaped her – like a mirror, almost. But her brain infarct made her realise that she was not herself, and she asked: 'Shall I ever feel whole again?'

It was the exact same question I was struggling with.

In the meantime, my normal life was starting to knock on the door again. I was invited to send over some pitches for stories to *The Times* newspaper to promote the memory events I'd organised at the Cheltenham Literature Festival. I composed one, and sent it over to a friend in Bermondsey, south London, for proofing. Within half an hour I received an alarming email back, with corrections to the text I'd sent over:

The Proust Phenomenon

Ever [TYPO CORRECTED] since Proust wrote the famous Madeleine episode 100 years ago, scientists have been investigatING [GRAMMAR CORRECTED] and trying to emulate Proust's experience. This article WILL [GRAMMAR CORRECTED] give some examples of what psychologists and neuroscientists have said about Proust, but it [TYPO CORRECTED] argues that the literary author still gives us THE [CORRECTED] finest insight into the human mind. Includes a ['cooking' DELETE] recipe to test one's senses.

In sixty-three words, I had made a litany of mistakes. I wrote *investigate* for *investigating*, used singular instead of plural nouns, and forgot a definite article. I wrote: 'the literary author still gives us *a* finest insight'. I wrote 'but *is* argues'. I even spelled the first word incorrectly (*even* for *ever*). Usually I'm attuned to spotting tautology, but 'cooking recipe' slipped through. I simply did not see these mistakes when I wrote this chunk. It was a disaster.

I was so ashamed of what was happening to me. I rang my friend in Bermondsey and begged him to help me get these pitches straight. Later I sent them over to the Festival Director, and rolled into bed, the blood buzzing in my head.

I didn't hear back from *The Times*, and I wasn't surprised in the least.

Although my speech was still impaired, swearing was not an issue – I was muttering curses in all three types of swearing: sexual, blasphemous and scatological. Besides these a lot of WTFs departed from my mouth. I took pleasure in the fact that a curse could express my frustration and bewilderment. Benjamin Bergen notes an interesting connection between brain damage and swearing, I learned:

We've known for a long time that specific parts of the brain play special roles in language. The critical bit of evidence is that when these certain parts of the brain suffer damage, due for instance to a stroke, lesion, or trauma, people start to have trouble pronouncing or understanding words. But the same brain damage leaves other cognitive capacities unaffected. This tells us that these particular brain regions are important for language. But there's a twist, and it involves profanity. Damage to language-supporting brain regions doesn't impair all language equally. In fact, a lot of the time, even when brain damage obliterates most language, swearing still remains. And people with brain damage do swear. A lot. (They do have a lot to swear about, what with the brain damage and all.)

This fact was interesting, and Bergen gives us a lot of information about the brain and language, especially for those who have lost their linguistic abilities: 'it means that the automatic, reflexive swearing that spurts out when you stub your toe or get cut off on the highway uses a different part of the brain from the rest of language. Language, we've come to find out, isn't all localized in the same place in the brain. [...] But we only know this because of the *shits* and *goddamnits* that leap from the mouths of people with brain damage who are otherwise linguistically challenged.'

Over a hundred years ago, it was Sigmund Freud who first made arguments against the localization of a motor and sensory aphasia as put forward by Broca and Wernicke, the guys whose discoveries were instrumental in my diagnosis. Freud become famous for his psychoanalytic theories, but in the last decade of the nineteenth century, he also published a number of neurological books. Of the brain regions pointed to by Broca and Wernicke after their observation of cerebral disturbances of speech, they had singled out the brain centre as being involved in the conception and production of language. In *On Aphasia*, Freud argued against rigid topographical explanations of the disorder, and was interested in investigating functional ones. He explained aphasia not by a localisation of the lesion (the specific place of the injury) but 'by conditions of reduced capacity for conduction in the apparatus of speech'. He argued that the brain consisted of 'contiguous cortical centres' – just like (a) memory wasn't localised, speech was a process making use of various regions of the brain, though it was perhaps orchestrated by one specific region. Freud thought of language as an interconnected rather than discrete system, which therefore could not be disconnected from other brain functions. He maintained that we need a more complicated presentation of the speech apparatus; he spoke of the 'free space of language', or the zone of language. He was against what was then the fashionable idea of brain centres – which still makes his work prescient, even visionary.

Freud went further, beyond 'speech', and spoke of a more extensive 'apparatus of expression'. Aphasia was about people not being able to communicate: a patient is considered aphasic not according to whether he or she can produce sounds, but whether the other people understand those utterances as meaningful. In Freud's vision, aphasia was not simply about brain injury, but it became about communication, and about the social dimension of human interaction. It was like the varying definitions of an alcoholic: you can diagnose someone as having a drinking problem by counting the number of drinks a person has, or by the time someone starts drinking in the day, or you can diagnose it by the problems drinking causes to the drinker and his social circle. For Freud the aphasic patient was someone who cannot communicate rather than someone incapable of expressing her or himself. There was to him a performative quality about aphasia, but also an expressive nature to language separate from its specific speech functions, because 'the problem lies in the "conventional" nature of the sign that is impaired in aphasia rather than an actual expression itself'.

Freud became a neuro-sceptic *avant la lettre*. His investigations into aphasia made it clear that the idea of localisation of speech in the brain was untenable. He saw that there were regions involved with the conceptualisation and production of language (the Broca and Wernicke areas as discussed earlier), but that the unique character of human language comes out of intricate operations that involve the brain as well as the mind. The explanation of how language works escapes neurological structures and analysis. Studies of the brain would in Freud's estimation also be unable to explain consciousness – this is the 'explanatory gap', the term that indicates the inability that materialist theories have in explaining human experience. Freud urged us to move beyond strictly neurological accounts when he realised the limits of neuro-psychological terms, and this opened up for him the complex relation between body and mind. He remained a materialist yet started to focus his attention on the mysteries of the human *psyche*. Language remained at the heart of Freud's *modus operandi*: it was the testimonies of his patients that could give access to an understanding of disease. This could be physical and mental – or a combination, as I had been experiencing myself.

A week after the first session of tapping my mind, I entered my shrink's Highgate office again. The clock stood behind him, its hands shoving me towards death. Impatience flared up – a feeling I wasn't unaccustomed to: I wanted to push on with my life. I had better things to do than talk about myself: finish new books, write my novel, teach my students, hang out with my friends, annoy my family, visit galleries and museums to ponder arty stuff, talk lofty philosophical ideas with my doctoral students.

But I couldn't. Two months ago, I had been mowed down in an existential drive-by shooting. I could barely write a proper sentence, and when I taught, I found myself stammering, looking for words, which no longer came easily. I was still exhausted and slept thirteen hours a day. I avoided people, and hardly saw my friends. My mind waged war against itself. I had mood swings, but mostly I was just down, empty. A darkness sat inside my body – a pot of black ink. My perception seemed permanently scrambled. I was no longer sure how to relate to other people and my emotions. I just felt a darkness.

Fury pounded inside. What had happened to me was unfair. This was not how my life was supposed to unfold.

Then my anger was joined by a third, contradictory emotion: a muted cheerfulness, a blasé *c'est la vie* feeling. Who cares about a small neurological defect? I survived, and in the scope of a lifetime of hardship this tiny bit of damage was nothing. I was lucky. I was alive. Rejoice! *Carpe diem.* Enjoy, cheers, *proost!* Next to those swirling feelings, I caught myself being surprised that I was glad to be back in my psychopomp's office, looking forward to talking about the ways in which my brush with death had affected me. The churning of conflicting feelings was perplexing – I was a riot of clashing emotions. Emotional dyscontrol, I remembered.

My shrink gave a recap of our last session, going over the entire history of myself in great detail. When he had asked me to give an overview of my life during our previous meeting, it struck me that he didn't take notes. Now he seemed to narrate the plot points of my life from memory, almost verbatim. It was an impressive feat, I thought, to produce this character sketch in so much detail without the aid of writing. I suspected that he'd made a memory palace of my life, a mnemonic trick that uses a visual system to remember extensive lists of items, facts or ideas.

My shrink said: 'And so then you are hit by an event that thrashes your sense of self. You heart shoots a blood clot into your brain, which gets stuck in the posterior region of the left frontal lobe. A small but important part of the brain is starved of oxygen.' He tapped the left side of his skull, saying, 'The brain damage has a profound effect upon your personal and professional life. The language production area in your brain is hit, for one. You suffer from aphasia, are unable to speak and write properly, which is particularly troubling because you're a lecturer in English literature. The infarct is especially ironical given that you're leading a project on memory, in which you collaborate on research with neuroscientists. Your mood and behaviour are affected as well. You swing from highs to lows, and you're depressed about your future. You experience many contradictory emotions, and feel locked up inside yourself. And you're dealing with a vast array of existential questions: the fact that you're mortal, that you have limits, that you are no longer young, that you are a contradictory human being with insecurities and emotions that make you vulnerable. The bright future you thought you had ahead of yourself is so much more uncertain now. And you also want to find out the cause of your infarct, but maybe there isn't one. Maybe it was a fluke, a quirk. That would be a hard pill to swallow for a person who seeks reasons and causes behind everything.'

My shrink cleared his throat as if to apologise for reminding me of my depression, and stated: 'Bas, thank you for being so candid about your thoughts and feelings last time we met. When I listened to you talk, last week, about your life and about the stroke episode, what struck me is that you are, or are behaving like, a rational person. The way you talk about yourself, it seems to me, is as if it concerns an altogether different person. You're talking about someone who isn't really you. You are objectifying yourself like a lab rat in a cage rather than thinking about yourself as a human being with feelings, doubts, and shortcomings.'

'You're not the first one to tell me this,' I noted.

His diagnosis-verdict continued: 'I think there are mainly three factors that have contributed to you having become aloof and overly cerebral. You are by nature a sensitive, shy boy, and the emotional turbulence that came with your unstable upbringing caused you to avoid investing your trust and emotions in other people immediately; you want to keep your distance before people can hurt you. Secondly, this caused you to flee towards rationality. You may have unconsciously chosen your academic career because this allowed you to continue your analytical attitude towards the world. I mean, you are attracted to the emotions and sensibilities that literature provides, but your approach to life itself is that of an intellectual. Everything has to be logical, make sense – and this academic attitude has become a habit that you use in all spheres of life. The third issue is the loss of José and your pregnancies, your potential children. The infertility trajectory has worn down your ability to feel emotions at all. You say you ended up feeling dead inside.'

My psychologist leaned forward, looked me in the eye and spoke further: 'What I think is important for you is to understand that your clinical approach cuts off a side of yourself that you require to be a rounded human being. You need to allow yourself a willingness to experience emotions, even though these make you feel vulnerable and bring uncertainties with them. You must learn to trust and rely on other people again. Be irrational, use your emotions to understand people, use your creative, counterintuitive instincts, which we both know you possess in abundance. Write your novel, write your screenplay – let go of your rational tendencies, and embrace your emotional brain. That is your task, and you can use your stroke event as an opportunity for bringing positive change to your character. You must reconnect with that lost side of yourself to rediscover the understanding of what life is really about, and to become at one with yourself again.'

Become at one with myself again, I thought, that sounds fantastic but how can I achieve that?

On the way back home, I was experiencing the first realisation that, despite this bleak, brutal understanding about life itself, what had happened to me was a source of great knowledge. Maybe I was giving re-birth to my former, younger self, and was also finding a new balance between the head and the heart. I had an inkling of this process, as I was starting to play music again: I picked up the guitar and wrote a song.

Perhaps the brain attack was becoming a revelation: the accident was disclosing the nature of my own machinations. The disruption of the flow of consciousness showed how the brain's normal functioning created human experience – a smooth story that had now been broken off, brutally. The destruction of a part of my brain was lifting the veil off new understandings – of my brain's (mal)functioning, my psychology, my relation to others, and of the very core of myself. The damage inside my brain was setting in motion a transformation of my personality – a new me that welded together the remains of my mature self with the childhood version of myself, a vulnerable, delicate boy who'd been roughed up by life.

Chapter Twelve
Writing Without Strange Blunders

The day came inevitably: I turned forty. Normally it would have been a cause for a party, but I was nearly killed six weeks ago so my mood was far from celebratory. And besides, I was working. I was in Gloucester, at the Cheltenham Literature Festival, where we'd organized four events for the memory project.

At the festival, the Director congratulated me and pointed to a fridge containing a bottle of champagne with my name on it. The first event went well. We were in a tent with two hundred semi-militant climate-change activists, talking about global warming and memory. The room buzzed with ideas generated by the three fully operative brains sitting next to me: a climate-change specialist, an ecocritic and a novelist. In front of me were two hundred electro-chemical batteries, and soon I grew tired, and my mind started to wander. A member of the audience shouted over the ecocritic, and, as Chair, I should have intervened, but I was too slow. By the time we were done, I was exhausted. The event was a disaster, I thought.

We retreated to the Green Room, and the Director congratulated me on the event's roaring success. She uncorked the champagne and handed me a birthday card. Flutes were passed along to the speakers and me, and we toasted my fortieth. We ate, drank and chatted, but I had already switched off. Their professorial brains were Duracell drummer bunnies that go on and on – my brain, the low-cost variety, had run out.

The next day, during breakfast, I chatted to Adam Roberts, who told me about the impact of Sir Walter Scott's brain infarct on his writing. On his phone he showed me an excerpt from Scott's diary entry of 5 April 1831:

> I have a hideous paralytic custom of stuttering with my pen, and cannot write without strange blunders; yet I cannot find any failure in my intellect.

Scott was nearing the end of his life, Roberts noted, and he'd suffered a big stroke with a severe diminution in his mental capacity and physical flexibility, which may partly have been attributed to the fact he needed to pay off his considerable debts. He had a financial interest in the Ballantyne printing business, which had collapsed because of a banking crisis in 1825. Rather than let himself be declared bankrupt, Scott was determined to write himself out of his debt. Already known as an obsessively prolific writer, he continued to produce many novels, as well as a biography of Napoleon Bonaparte. Scott's manuscripts hardly contained any punctuation marks, and read like *Mrs Dalloway*'s stream-of-consciousness. His publisher, Robert Cadell, and his son-in-law, J. G. Lockhart, tried to correct the writing as much as possible, but they had a hard time with his final novels, *Castle Dangerous* and *Count Robert of Paris*, both published in 1832. The novels were wild rivers of prose, and make for a very strange, surreal reading experience. Scholars have tried to establish what was really Scott's writing, and what were the editorial interventions, attempting to rescue the mad outpouring of ink. The Journal, which he wrote between 1825 and 1832, when his life ended after a series of strokes, is shockingly difficult to decipher. The diary ends mid-sentence *en route* from Naples to Rome on 16 April: 'We slept reasonably, but on the next morning'...

There wasn't to be a next morning for Scott. A day before his death, Scott penned a sketch for a novella, which was published posthumously as 'The Death of Il Bizarro', the protagonist being the captain of a gang of bandits, named for his wily yet inexorable temper. They were the final 847 words if his oeuvre, which comprised more than twenty-six novels, twelve poetry collections, plays and a wealth of non-fiction works. I wondered about the mind of Scott, and the brain that generated his immense literary achievements. His addiction to writing was striking. Never give up! Write till you die.

Later that day at the festival, we staged a panel discussion about the Proust Phenomenon, the fact that smells can trigger emotional childhood memories. A Scottish philosopher hosted a panel debate with a novelist, a psychologist who worked with me at my University, and a Professor of Cultural Cognition. I was glad I didn't have to chair this session – I didn't want to stumble and stutter again, as I'd perceived of my hosting the previous night. I wanted to take my usual two-hour afternoon nap, but it was impossible in the Green Room. Around me were historians, television presenters, writers, TV gardeners and celebrity chefs – all so alive, energetic: their brains were magnets, force fields pulling me each and every way – it was dizzying. I plugged in my earphones, put on Maria João Pires' Schubert record, and went for a walk whilst grey clouds blew over me. I was walking away, literally, from the events that I'd organised – and I didn't care.

On the train back to London, the intense conversation between the Scottish philosopher and my psychologist colleague wore me out. The philosopher told me he had been keeping a close eye on me and was concerned. He could hear the effects of the stroke in my speech, he told me: I spoke slower, was searching for words. I found an empty seat in the back and tried to sleep. Through the gap between the seats in front of me, I looked at the philosopher gesticulating, watching his mouth produce words fluently as if it didn't cost him the least bit of effort. *The brainsick words of rhetoricians, they flow forth from my mouth veritably and freely.* (Too much alliteration, Joyce!) I wondered how, if at all, I would ever be able to regain my rhetorical skills. Outside the compartment window, fields, sheep and trees covered by black shadows whizzed by, which I watched until I was fast asleep.

The next day, a month or so after the stroke event, I was on the overground once again, gliding back to the Royal Free Hospital. I contemplated the happiness-list that my psychologist had asked me to create at the end of my last session. I had a go at this and pondered the results:

1. Writing.
2. Sports.
3. Gigs.
4. Gardening.
5. Having fun with children.
6. Skiing.
7. Sitting on piazzas in European cities or hotel balconies, watching people.
8. Reading.
9. Making love.
10. Sitting in the sun with a glass of wine, chatting or just doing nothing.
11. Live classical music.
12. Walking.
13. Playing guitar, playing with my band.
14. Travel.
15. Food. Good food.

'Having fun with children'… that sounded a bit creepy, but I understood why my shrink had asked me to do this. It was easy to disappear into a depression. The list put my life into perspective. It forced me to acknowledge that I was extremely lucky. That there was hope. But it was also telling me to appreciate and enjoy the little things in life.

In the waiting room of the Cardiology Department, I sat amongst the predominantly elderly crowd, some anxious and silent, looking frail but cheerful, some chatting on their phones or tapping on their screens, joking with the staff. I was irritated by yet another investigation. It swallowed up so much time that I knew I couldn't retrieve.

NHS hospital waiting rooms often have daytime television on, the volume unnecessarily loud. At some point, someone in top management must have decided that the noise the TV creates is the best means of distraction for people who are worrying. I'd never seen such a psychological tactic outside the UK. In continental Europe, there are magazines and music. Most of the time people are simply left to contemplate their existential angst in aggravating silence.

To drown out my anxious thoughts, I let Britten's Cello Suites stream into my ears. It is the saddest instrument, the cello, and the Britten pieces are deeply melancholic. These suites felt so alone. The high-pitched notes, inconsolable screeches of despair, and the low dark sonorous noises, melancholic. I was unconsciously choosing these pieces as they reflected my mood, but the effect wasn't helping my emotional stability.

I was collected by a young nurse with a Scottish accent. We entered what to me seemed a storage cupboard, and she explained the procedure. She showed me the Holter monitor, a device the size of a mobile phone which she would clip onto my trousers. The device would be connected to four electrodes, which she would glue and tape to my chest. She shaved my chest hair and connected the electrodes to my torso, checked if the device was recording, and sent me on my way.

On the train back, I thought about how the rhythms of my life had changed drastically – how out of sync I was. I felt the Holter monitor on my chest, recording my body's dynamo. The average heart beats about eighty times per minute, which means that at forty years of age it has beaten a tremendous number of times. I had been in this world for about 21,024,400 minutes (leap years included), and my heart had beaten, I reckoned, 1,681,920,000 times. No wonder that something may have gone wrong. A skipped beat, a slow beat, a double beat – a cardiological hop, step and jump. Maybe my heart, that fateful night last August, forgot to beat for a few seconds and my blood cells started to clot together, and my heart fired this cluster of cells into my brain.

In the bathroom at night, I looked at the heart monitor clasped to my shorts, its wires grabbing my chest: through these electrodes tiny electrical pulses were running from the heart, creating an archive that my neurologist would decode. There was no difference between the body's electricity and the currents running through the device. This apparatus and I had become one: I was a cyborg. I wished I were infallible like a machine, able to be repaired and brought back to a state of perfection. But this wasn't possible: I was a human being, imperfect, fragile, with a body that would grow weaker and weaker.

I realised my life was turning out very differently from what I had imagined ten or twenty years ago. The warm, all-encompassing joy I had felt when looking into the future was now cold, dead. My life lacked the ingredients for gratifying fullness: intelligence without smartness, too much brain, not enough heart. As punishment I dreamt of endless visits to London hospitals with José, and black-and-white screens showing no heartbeats, nothing, just static.

Whilst wearing the Holter device I continued my investigation into the connection between the stroke and my impaired language. Although I did not know much about it myself, I was aware that recently Humanities scholars had started to use computers and artificial intelligence to understand language. I wondered if the use of machine-learning, a sub-branch of AI, may yield insight into my stroke's effects. Machine learning made use of computers to study statistics and algorithms without giving them a specific set of instructions: the computer detects patterns within the data and builds an analysis rather than looking for specific preset goals.

I contacted a colleague who worked in Computational Linguistics. I wondered whether she would be able to tell the ways in which my language had changed if I supplied her with a lot of my email correspondence and academic writing from 2003 up to the stroke event and similar source material from the stroke onwards. She said she might. Maybe.

I collated texts from various email accounts, and drafts of essays and books and short stories, amounting to a novel-length collection of writing. The digital wizard used about 150 emails written in English from just before and after my stroke as so-called 'training data'. She unleashed a number of different algorithms and 'features' on the text files to see if there were any significant changes in my writing before and after my stroke. She would use tools to generate out of my writing a probabilistic model for predicting items in a sequence. Let's say that to the phrase 'I hope all's ...' you will probably append the word 'well' rather than 'elephant'. We see this prediction of words on our phones and in email systems all the time: the software is anticipating what words are used as a general rule. The more advanced this technology becomes, the more potentially personal to the individual user the predictions may be. Predictive modelling could create a kind of blueprint of how an individual uses language.

It took a bit for my head to get around what she was doing exactly, and why, but I understood that as a computational linguist she was breaking down my language and style in a subtle way so that she could arrive at some kind of mathematical function, which could then be compared to the training data so that we could tell whether – perhaps – the 'rules' of my vocabulary and grammar had changed after my stroke.

I was in for a disappointment. She wrote back to say that the results were not very exciting. There seemingly wasn't much difference in my language before and after my stroke, even though it seemed to me that my spelling and grammar had certainly become messier.

We concluded that the form of my language, the grammar and spelling, had on the whole not changed dramatically after my stroke but what had changed were the topics of my writing. Though in the files that the linguist sent me, I saw plenty of evidence of my misspellings:

comitted
proabbly
goign
generla
fudning
flyinjg

billingual
abaility

It wasn't clear whether these were simply traces of haste or the results of the stroke, but the linguist could not say anything conclusive to suggest that the internal structure of my language-use had (or had not) changed in itself. We needed more data, more emails, though the assembly of a corpus was a precise matter and the linguist warned me that I might have to put in a lot of work for little gain. I decided to leave this avenue of investigation. It seemed a dead end.

The relationship between data, digital technology and language led to another discovery. I found out that the late king of cyberpunk, the writer Philip K. Dick, had survived stroke. I knew Dick's work. On my *Literature in the Digital Age* course I was teaching his classic SF novel *Do Androids Dream of Electric Sheep?*, a book in which humans hunt robots ('replicants') that are able to fake the traits that make humans human: empathy and memory. Dick imagined that in the future we would end up in a situation in which we could no longer tell the difference between humans and pre-programmed humanoids that would think and feel just like us.

Dick had suffered a series of minor strokes in the early 1970s. He was a prolific writer, a visionary who wrote some of today's SF classics, and numerous other stories and novels that were subsequently adapted into successful films such as *Total Recall* and *Minority Report*. His personal life was wild if not outrageous: he married five times, experimented with drugs and experienced hallucinations and paranormal experiences. Dick had visions of God, which triggered various nervous breakdowns and an attempted suicide. He claimed he was guided by a 'spirit'. Combined with sky-rocketing blood pressure, these breakdowns and visions took a severe toll on his mind and body, resulting in a series of brain infarcts. His wife noted in a letter:

The times I think of as 'minor strokes' are the times when he stumbled for no apparent reason, when he suddenly turned livid or flushed, when he would blank-out in mid-sentence. These were stressful times, and I believe he was having strokes, although very minor ones. If the spirit had not told him to go to the doctor, he might have died.

Dick kept on writing, including *A Scanner Darkly*, turned into an animated movie with Keanu Reeves, and *Valis*. Early in 1982, he was interviewed by a journalist, but he complained afterwards of failing eyesight. This time the spirit was not present to tell him to see a doctor, or if it was he did not listen. The next day he was found unconscious, having suffered a big stroke. In hospital he suffered another debilitating attack, after which his heart failed and brain activity diminished rapidly. He died five days later, aged 53. In that final interview, Dick stated: 'I wanted to write about a guy who pushes his brain to its limits, is aware he has reached his limit, but voluntarily decides to go on and pay the consequences.'

I pondered the life of this visionary berserker. Did I want to be that guy – a tragic, tragically unshakable anti-hero, a stubborn fool who decides to go on and on until his dying breath? A former boss once spoke of my 'single-minded' determination but I was no longer sure that I liked that characteristic.

Once again I was on my way to the Royal Free Hospital. I'd slept badly because of the Holter monitor. I kept tossing and turning, and woke up frazzled. After a month of doing the blood tests, the results hadn't arrived, though I was led to believe they would be known within a week. The longer the wait, the more frustrated and anxious I became. After three weeks, I rang and emailed various people at the Royal Free, and finally got hold of an Operational Manager who told me that the results were indeed in the system. It was unclear if the results had gone to my neurologist and GP. Maybe they'd been lost? I said I'd happily collect a print-out, a request to which the Operational Manager agreed.

In the foyer of the Royal Free I was handed a brown envelope with the results and an apology by the manager. My neurologist would write to me immediately explaining the results, she said. I asked her if she could look at the documents right then and there but she noted that she wasn't 'medical'. I thanked her and fled the dead hospital smell.

At the Hampstead overground station, I could no longer contain my curiosity and opened the envelope. It contained sheets of paper with lists – but not Happiness Lists. The first sheet contained information about rare genetic disorders that might have made my blood clot. The General Haematology results reported on Haematocrit, the Neutrophil Count, the White Blood Count and Erythrocyte Sedimentation Rate. The Haematology was followed by the General Biochemistry of my blood, which contained 143 millimol *Sodium* (salt) per litre, 4.3 mmol *Potassium* (mix with chloride if you're on a killing spree), *Urea Serum* (sounded like a planet from a science fiction novel) and 87 umol/L of *Creatinine*. I didn't understand these strange terms but they made my blood magical and mysterious.

On the train, I went over the rest of the report and the lists of examinations of the Coagulation and Autoimmune Serology:

APTT 50/50 mix
American Diagnostic DVVC
Lupus Anticoagulent Index
Activated Protein C Resistance
Prothrombin 20210 Gene Screen
Factor V Leiden Genotype
Anti Nuclear antibody (Hep 2)
ENA Screen
dsDNA ELISA
Anti-Neutrophil Cytoplasmic Ab
Cardiolipin IgG Antibody

These tests were performed to see how quickly my blood coagulates. I presumed that if my blood coagulated too fast, there was an increased risk of blood clots. The Factor V Leiden was a genetic disorder, so Google told me, that causes an increase in blood clotting with the tendency to form abnormal blood clots. Prothrombin 20210 was a test for a mutation within the prothrombin gene where, at position 20210 of the DNA, the adenine (A) is substituted by a guanine (G). A single glitch in your DNA could make your blood coagulate too fast, leading potentially to deep vein thrombosis and pulmonary embolism, a blockage in the artery in the lungs by a clot that has travelled a long way. ELISA turned out to be the abbreviation of 'enzyme-linked immunosorbent assay', a test that uses antibodies and colour-change to identify antigens – molecules capable of inducing an immune response. In short, an antigen is a substance that causes an immune system to produce antibodies against your own body. Anti-Neutrophil Cytoplasmic Ab was a group of autoantibodies which fight antigens and might trigger your body to fight against itself.

The lists with their cascade of unfamiliar words kept on coming and they sucked the energy out of me. Yet, as far as I could tell, all of the results were marked either Negative, Normal, Not Applicable, or had numbers behind them. Quickly I did some Googling and to me it seemed as if everything was fine. This was a relief. I texted my mother and sent through some pictures of the documents. My mind was set at ease: my blood wasn't the cause of the stroke. Perhaps it was my heart?

Once I was satisfied I'd made sense of the medical terms I made photocopies and brought the originals over to my GP, and set up an appointment to go over them to ensure that the results were indeed fine. A few days later, I received an apologetic letter from my neurologist, which confirmed that everything was in order. It was a relief but the letter turned out to be useless. It stated 'The cholesterol was 3.4' but did not explain that this is well below the danger threshold of 5; I had to Google this. It also reported: 'Your ANA, ANCA, ENA, double stranded DNA and anticardiolipin antibodies were all also normal.' These abbreviations and terms meant nothing to me. The letter stated that they were awaiting the result of the Fabry's analysis, but I didn't know what this was.

The internet told me it was a rare genetic lysomal storage disease causing a wide range of symptoms, and, amongst others, had cerebrovascular effects that sometimes lead to stroke.

A couple of weeks later my GP confirmed that there was absolutely nothing wrong with my blood. No genetic disease, no hidden predisposition to clotting. The results of the Holter heart monitor had come back without anything of interest as well. It looked like the stroke was just stupid bad luck. The only thing we could do was to try a longer, three-day Holter test. It was all deeply dissatisfying. I wanted to know why the stroke happened but medicine seemed unable to explain.

My craving for meaning increased even further. I felt powerless against what had happened to me, and powerless against what might come.

To cope with such doubts and uncertainties, I decided to go to my psychologist again. I told him about another touchstone for my experience that had come to me whilst on a long walk. This was Rebecca West's novel *The Return of the Soldier*, which tells the story of a rational and upper-class soldier, Chris Baldry, and his shallow wife, Kitty, who'd lost their son, Oliver. This traumatic experience had hardened them both and they grew apart. Chris returns from the front after the Great War, shell-shocked and suffering from memory loss. Shell-shock is what we now call post-traumatic stress syndrome, and the aftermath of my stroke was not dissimilar to this, I felt: trauma is trauma. Although he is in his thirties, the shell-shock caused by the war makes him think he is twenty years old again: he reverts to a former, more innocent version of himself – emotional, open, a genuinely nice person. Even his appearance changes – he comes across as a young and sprightly man. He starts writing love letters to a woman he had an affair with during his youth. She turns up and they continue their earlier relationship under the watchful eye of a psychoanalyst. They are happy once more, though his wife feels rejected by him. Due to a physical head injury, the older and rational Chris re-emerges – this is the second 'return of the soldier' – and Kitty is delighted to have her 'old' husband back. "'He's cured'" she exclaims, but it's clear that Chris has reverted to his mature, unhappier self. The 'happy' ending is ironic.

I reminded myself that my own stroke event had caused a state of shock, which was lingering. Brain injury was like the wounds caused by war: 'patients with brain lesions, behave as if they are suffering from *war trauma'* a philosopher had written. Even though there was no wound visible, any shock, or any strong psychological stress or anxiety, impacts the emotional brain, an unrecognised part of human beings. If you want to connect your ideas of the brain and the mind up properly, you must look into the nature of the emotional brain that gives us our secret, unconscious life of feelings and drives that determine who we are.

What struck me was that this was a question of fate. Now that it was slowly becoming clear that there was no identifiable cause behind the stroke, that there were no clear constitutional factors that had provoked the brain attack, I had to accept that the infarct was a pure accident. The wound in my brain tissue showed me the absence of sense, of a clear meaning of the stroke. How could I come to terms with its violence if there was no reason for it in the first place?

'There is another way of looking at your stroke,' my shrink noted. 'The stroke has been a destructive event, for sure. It has hit you in the brain, and it has killed off a certain version of you. A person who chased a career, who needed recognition for his achievements. But consider this: you can see your stroke not only as an act of destruction, but perhaps it is also an event that is creative. The stroke shows that the plasticity of your brain – and your psychology – offers you the possibility of being transformed without being destroyed. To avoid annihilation, your brain is adapting, modifying itself – and your personality is as well. So, the brain attack is a form of freedom from fixity of character. You are able to change and escape the imprisonment of the psychic make-up that you had built for yourself. You are free. Free to change. Free to revert to your former self, and create a new you. Are you ready for that?'

Walking back to my home, I understood I was staring at a dilemma. During the session with my shrink I saw that by evoking the stories of Kafka and West I was deflecting. Using stories about other, fictional people was a roundabout way to understand my own situation. Why was I so afraid of directly confronting my own situation? Maybe it was just too confusing, too scary to address head-on. I was trying to cope with trauma and was alienated by the medical machinery with its unfamilliar language, so fell back on my academic expertise to make sense of my predicament. In the first place it was literature that offered meaning and comfort. Stories were the mirror that allowed me to see in the darkness. But my knowledge about the brain and memory too was something that stood me in great stead as it helped me understand the emotional turmoil and the layerings of personality that seemed to struggle with one another. I was unsure how to unite these two aspects of my life, literature and science, as I had been trying to do before my stroke. And I was no longer sure if this would be enough to get me through my recovery.

I saw a choice: to accept confinement in the constructed identity of myself as an academic, or to accept the possibility of exploring new, potentially dangerous but liberating freedoms that would allow the search for a new way of living. The latter prospect filled me with terror and excitement in equal measure – and when I closed my eyes I could see a glimmer of possibility, the promise of transformation. Yes, I could also choose the safer option and retrench in the security of my identity as a scholar and lock myself in my study again. But I saw this choice was an opportunity, which offered me the chance to regain control over my life. I needed to break out of my depression and self-absorption. I realised I hadn't left my neighbourhood for three months. I was stuck, mentally and physically, and I needed to explore the possibility of finding a new way of living, even if this more dangerous option could inflict more damage.

At that moment I understood that I needed to embark on a journey of discovery and learning in order to cure my wounded head and carve out a new self. Even though I knew this plan seemed impetuous and dangerous, the urge to embark on such a quest was irresistible. If I made the wrong decision, I could lose everything.

In my mind, a new plan was taking shape – a novel future. I could see the outlines, vaguely. Its proposition seemed hazardous and went against the advice of my doctors and friends, yet the urge to explore this potential new road – a new life – was irresistible.

Part III
An Odyssey of Maybes

Chapter Thirteen
And I Shall Need All My Brains to Get Through

It was November, three months after the attack, and I was being pulled into two contradictory directions. I had seen the possibility of living a new, less careerist life, but the urge to pretend that nothing was the matter with me was just as strong. I was ignoring the undeniable fact that ten or so weeks ago I'd had a stroke that had changed my personality, my behaviour, and my ability to write properly. A depression had me in its grip: I was avoiding people, and I was lethargic. The accident had hit my confidence in myself, and I was struggling with questions and doubts about who I was, what life I had been leading. But I was also anxious about the life that lay ahead of me, as an aphasic literature professor.

So, what do you do, as a stupid bloke? You deny what has happened, and pretend nothing is wrong. I was trying to fool my doctors, my shrink, my family and friends, my colleagues, and not least myself. In fact, I was redoubling my efforts to paint a picture of myself as a cool dude who could not be destroyed by anything, not even by an attack on his brain.

So I continued work as if nothing happened. A colleague in Malaysia and I had been organising a conference on the state of memory in the twenty-first century in Kuala Lumpur, just before Christmas. My partners in KL and I had been working on the conference for a while; there was grant money; and we'd already attracted delegates the world over. Surely, we couldn't cancel such an amazing event for a little brain trauma? Even if my neurologist had forbidden long-haul flights and stressful circumstances.

It would have been sensible to have given myself a break but instead I followed my GP's advice and got on with it, sipping royally from my KEEP CALM AND CARRY ON mug, pretending I was alright – which I wasn't. This was self-affirmation, projecting an image onto the outside world to show I was still as tireless and creative as before. But I was acting this version of myself; in fact, I was overacting.

Things were far from okay, though. On the outbound flight to Malaysia, I was deeply anxious. The neurologist had told me to walk around every so often in order to prevent thrombosis, which causes blood clots. This normally happens to elderly people but I was now at risk. It was an overnight flight, so I walked around the plane whilst the rest of the five hundred passengers were sleeping. On the in-flight entertainment I found a Malaysian film, *Anak Halal*, meaning *Holy Child*, which gave me an idea for an essay. I started writing right then and there. My brain was firing on all cylinders, all the way through the night, up in the stratosphere. Just before we landed, I had finished my paper, 'Tiger Literature: Theory and Practice in Fiction of Rising Power Nations'. My writing was getting better now. I still made some spelling and grammatical mistakes, though:

The film at various point suggest visually

In Tash Aw's *Five Star Billionaire*, for many of the characters, there move to Shanghai is

Ouch.

But on the whole this paper read well: there were relatively well composed but (over)long sentences, some signs of original ideas about this new genre of literature, and plenty of dead academic jargon. I was regaining some confidence in my writing ability. Indeed, the actual process of sustained writing and editing – which forced me to look close-up at my language – was helping me move forward with my aphasia.

And I Shall Need All My Brains to Get Through

The conference and my paper were a success. Afterwards I had a great time with one of my best friends who lived in Kuala Lumpur, drinking pool-side cocktails, and enjoying Malaysian food, which reminded me of the Indonesian cuisine I knew so well from José and her family. Malaysia was triggering sensory memories of my wife and her culture. On a couple of occasions I explored the Kuala Lumpur city centre, and continued an earlier urban walking project with my Malaysian colleagues. I was trying to master the metropolis by hiking an ambulatory map of it into my brain: I was mending my brain by walking, recalibrating my inner compass, setting it to a new course.

I touched down in the UK on Christmas Day and had the loneliest Christmas I ever hope to experience. My mother tried to get me to come over to Holland, but I refused. I didn't want to travel again.

I felt uplifted by the thought that my personality was changing. I was taking more time to relax. Late one night, I rang José, and told her about my journey to Kuala Lumpur, saying it had changed me. I told her I was a different person now: thoughtful, less rushed, more loving and caring. She was surprised but happy and wanted to meet in the next few weeks.

As usual I cherished the special time between Christmas and New Year: the dead days, when time is no longer the rational clock time of the ordinary world but drifts by, slow and muted like snow. To recover from the jet lag I read a bit, watched films and box sets. I slept a lot, though not as long and deep as after the stroke. I met up for a pint with one of my best friends in The Lamb, a pub on Holloway Road. I told him about how I had experienced the turbulent aftermath of the stroke, and that I felt so different about so many things.

I spent New Year's Eve with another friend of mine. We drank a cocktail in a bar near Borough Market and ended up having dinner at a Spanish restaurant in Bermondsey Street. I told him that I was changing. He was pleased for me, but also sceptical.

'We'll see about that,' he said. 'People don't change, y'know.'

I said, 'Yes, I hear you. You may be right.' Real change emerges over a longer period of time, I know, and happens in a zig-zag kind of way; there never is a direct, straightforward path.

The optimism that had lifted me up and carried me through the final days of the year of my stroke dissipated rapidly at the start of the new year, though. The weather was miserable: low-hanging, rain-bearing clouds pushed down on the city and on my mind. The sky threatened to drown me; I felt lonely but I continued to isolate myself.

I met with two curators at the Whitechapel Gallery. They were planning an exhibition on the French film maker Chris Marker, who had recently died. Since Marker was obsessed by memory, the Gallery wanted to collaborate with the Memory Network by organizing two symposia bringing together renowned Marker scholars.

Four months after the stroke, I was back on my full teaching load. My Head of Department wanted to see me. She was concerned about my marking. The colleague who has been looking over my essays for *Poetics of Surveillance* had brought to her attention that my spelling and grammar were very poor. I needed to address this as soon as possible. I needed to correct my feedback before the work was released to the students. She suggested I move to audio feedback for the time being so I could record my feedback verbally. The Department would order a headset for me.

I apologised and made my way out of the office feeling dizzy. The problem was that often I did not see my mistakes. I had to reread everything twice and unleash the spell-checker before I sent messages. This was bad, and I felt everything could go wrong again.

Over the next days, I reworked my student feedback to the best of my ability. I also went for long walks in the January cold through the Queen's Wood and Hampstead Heath, trying to stem the panic that sometimes reared up inside me.

Over the weekend I had New Year's drinks with friends, but my spelling and grammar mistakes were on my mind. I cursed myself for not having asked for the entire semester off.

It would have been reasonable to give myself a complete rest for three months after a brain attack.

And I noticed that I was really out of sorts. No longer in control of my emotions, I fluctuated between lows that crippled my mind, and highs that I used to convince myself everything was alright. I frantically wrote a conference paper in six hours on the flight to Kuala Lumpur to suggest – to myself – that all would be well. And now I was set to fly to the States to give a paper at Yale University and visit East Coast universities to enlist colleagues in the Memory Network.

In the last week of January, my Department held its Exam Board, the meeting where students' grades are reviewed. My colleagues approached me with questions about my health. Someone made a wry remark about my fancy Malaysian trip, which I totally got. During the meeting, I didn't say much, afraid of stuttering and making mistakes. The grades for my modules were approved, and the surveillance course was praised for its innovation. I left the room as soon as we were finished.

I wrote to my neurologist to ask again if it was possible to have therapy to ameliorate the effects of my aphasia. The letter I got back stated that any therapy would be unlikely to have a significant effect on my performance. The NHS was under pressure; there was a long waiting list for post-stroke therapy and, frankly, he said, my condition was not so bad compared to other cases: no permanent physical complications. That's true, I thought, if only I weren't someone who teaches literature. I also knew that research into brain plasticity and rehabilitation in stroke patients had shown that for optimal recovery of the brain to take place the neural plasticity and therapeutic interventions need to be fine-tuned. There were defined 'plastic time windows' during which rehabilitation could be optimised – once the window is shut, it's shut. And I suspected the window of opportunity has already closed.

The Holter monitor I wore in November had yielded nothing: my heart was doing its job diligently. Though I thought this was just for show, my neurologist had one final line of investigation: I would have to wear the Holter monitor for three consecutive days. So, I visited the Royal Free Hospital again. A Caribbean nurse scraped away my chest hair this time. I said that I would have to wear the device for seventy-two hours. She tutted and said that's impossible. The Holter monitor can only record for forty-eight hours max. I found it strange that my neurologist didn't know the maximum recording length of a Holter monitor.

I wore the machine for two days but I knew it was useless. My heart was fine, and so was my blood. It wasn't divine punishment for my sins, nor was it caused by work stress or other behaviour. There was no genetic defect that caused my blood to clot and my heart is strong and reliable. My stroke was simply bad luck. I needed to accept this, but I didn't know if I could: I wanted a cause, a reason for my neuronal jamming. I didn't think I could accept this lack of knowledge about my infarct, that a random glitch in the wiring of my brain had resulted in this ongoing catastrophe. But I had to: my task now was to find a way of living with this absence of a clear cause.

In the final week of January, I spent more time on campus. One colleague cornered me to let me know that my absence had become conspicuous; he was wondering if I was doing alright – was there anything he could do? Some colleagues thought I'd deserted the Department. I said I was feeling better, that I needed time. Another colleague mentioned that it was likely that Tolstoy had a series of TIAs, smaller strokes that are less debilitating than full strokes, towards the end of his life. His excessive behaviour had become even more extravagant, and his language seemed different from before. He got very strange – and even underwent a religious conversion in old age. I added Tolstoy to my list of stroke-surviving writers.

In February, I co-taught a seminar on a Gothic course; the novel was *Dracula*. Bram Stoker died, I learned, after a series of debilitating stokes on 20 April 1912. The seminar became a traumatising experience. I dissected a long passage from Jonathan Harker's Journal in front of twenty-seven students. My brain glitched: I stumbled over words, stammered and stuttered through the passage, 'feeling as though my own brain were unhinged or as if the shock had come which must end in its undoing', and finished it, red-faced. Usually an animated reader, my confidence was now lost, blundering through this series of words incoherently, as if Stoker had put them together randomly. Harker seemed to speak to me when he said: 'I am, I know, either being deceived, like a baby, by my own fears, or else I am in desperate straits; and if the latter be so, I need, and shall need, all my brains to get through.' But I no longer have all my brains.

I was longing for some kind of normality; I was sick of my self-isolation. I couldn't wait for springtime to come, so I could get the garden ready for sowing and planting. Life was springing up in my incubators; my aim was to grow an early crop of tomatoes, spinach and courgettes. In May, I'd be able to harvest my elephant garlic and red onions. The thought of producing my own food filled me with delight. The boy from the farmer's village, who once drank warm frothy milk straight from the cow's teat, had not left me despite having lived in London's sprawling artifice for over ten years.

In the British Library I learned that Leo Tolstoy suffered from what Tolstoy's biographer Rosamund Bartlett calls 'Russian maximalist tendencies': he was a larger-than-life figure who lived his life, to employ the cliché, to the max. The young Tolstoy, already a rich landowner, was a gambler and a philanderer: he squandered 'his inheritance on gypsy singers and gambling. Whole villages were sold off to pay for his debt.' He wrote like he lived: grand, epic, explosive. This early bacchanalian spirit was countered by a Christian asceticism in later life. Indeed, the later Tolstoy paved the way for Communism by renouncing money and his private property, after he had become the embodiment of an emerging modern Russia. Like Dickens, Tolstoy was an avid walker with a nomadic spirit; they called him a *strannik*, which designated a member of a sect who went on pilgrimages from one monastery to another.

In Tolstoy's masterpiece, *War and Peace*, Prince Bolkonski has a stroke. The literary critic R. L. Albin argues that this brain attack is symbolic of wider developments in Russian society in the nineteenth century: the gradual rejection of the Enlightenment principles that underpinned the power of the Russian political elite. As a figure representing the elite, Bolkonski is suffering from a dementing process because of his stroke, which, Albin notes, is a metaphorical criticism, of 'the rationalistic, Western-influenced aristocracy that dominated Russia at the end of the 18th century. Prince Bolkonski's decline and apoplectic death parallel the fate of Enlightenment thought in Eastern Europe.' Just like *Tristram Shandy* and *Frankenstein*, *War and Peace* anticipates the demise of the Enlightenment and its belief in rationality and calculation as a way of understanding the world. The brain is a metaphor for pure reason and stroke symbolic of the malfunctioning that is bound to happen. To understand society Tolstoy knew that we need to acknowledge the role emotions and spirituality play in people's lives. This is not to say we need to submit to the irrational side of human behaviour; but we need to understand that in society the head and the heart are in a continuous struggle.

Over a hundred years later, my own stroke had given me the same lesson: it seemed to me that a century later our 'modern' society – plagued by fake news – was still embroiled in the same conflict. Perhaps this meant there was no moral or intellectual progress, but I did conclude that there was a continuity between the lives of people across countries and ages. The same human struggles kept on playing themselves out.

In 1908, Tolstoy suffered a series of minor strokes and developed phlebitis, an inflammation of the veins of his legs. By 1908, Russia's literary hero was bedridden and drafting his will. He stated that the copyright to all of his works was to be terminated upon his death. A year later, Tolstoy suffered another stroke after being accosted by thousands of ecstatic fans. He never fully recovered and would spend the final year of his life in a state of delirium and mental instability. His health rapidly deteriorated. This was exacerbated by his dysfunctional home life, which had almost completely crumbled. A year later, he suffered a mental breakdown. In November 1910, he fled his home, boarding a train in the dead of night. He would not survive the journey, succumbing to pneumonia in a train station while fleeing from the life he had failed to find.

It reminded me of my own quest for a new life – and Tolstoy's ending made my desire to discover it all the more urgent. I wondered how Tolstoy had felt when he realised he was going to die, knowing he was the one of the greatest writers his country had ever produced and that, although he was loved by his people, he hadn't quite managed to get to the place he had imagined. He hadn't died in peace.

This realisation for me was a turning point. I started to re-assess my own goals in life. Two academic milestones that I needed to achieve were the completion of two books I had been working on: a book on literature from the sixties, which I'd started and abandoned a number of times, as well as the editing of a gigantic book on memory. I made a plan to finish the sixties book slowly by giving myself two years to work on the individual chapters. The book on memory was currently too large a project to handle by myself: it contained forty-two chapters and was over 200,000 words – the size of three novels. I asked a number of friends and colleagues to help me work on the project. By sharing the burden the work would be more manageable for all involved. My request was accepted. I felt humbled by their caring gesture towards me.

I had a session with my shrink but I really no longer wanted to talk about death and my psychological problems; it was just another obstacle that slowed me and my recovery down. Our sessions had helped me to reflect on my condition, but I felt too much contemplation led to excessive self-scrutiny, which exacerbated my inward turn. 'I must connect with people,' I told him, 'or else I'll disappear into this dark hole of narcissistic introspection.' *I* wasn't important. I needed to focus on other people, my students, society – to make lives better.

'I understand,' he said. 'How are you feeling?' The dreaded question. I shrugged my shoulders and told him I thought major problems were coming my way. I no longer fitted in at work, didn't show up for meetings and wasn't communicating with colleagues; my writing was still seriously affected; I felt cut off from my friends and family even though it was I who was creating this situation; I was planning a work trip to the States, even though I wasn't sure why I was doing all this anymore. I was distrustful of my motivations.

We talked about the fact that science was unlikely to explain the cause of my stroke, which created a lot of uncertainty for my future. I was trying to find ways to make sense of my brain meltdown and, like a proper academic, I was reaching out to theories that were current. In *The Black Swan*, Nassib Taleb shows that the world has become increasingly unstable because of its growing economic interconnection. A small event in one part of the world can have a massive and not necessarily predictable impact on the other side of the world, as the assassination of the Archduke Franz Ferdinand triggered the First World War, with millions dead. Or the tremendous global consequences of the Wall Street Crash of 1929. Or a tiny virus from China that paralysed the entire world for two years. Such events were incredibly difficult to foresee. This makes our world fragile.

Taleb's theory showed how many aspects of our globalized world (don't) work in reality. I compared my stroke to a black swan: this tiny event in an incredibly small part of my brain had a huge impact upon my life, psychology and language. A neuroscientist spoke about 'global neuronal workspace', the 'global information broadcasting within the cortex: it arises from a neuronal network whose raison d'être is the massive sharing of pertinent information throughout the brain'. The neuronal black swan had impacted not just on me but on the immediate world around me: my social and professional eco-system were also suffering from the fall-out. My wife, friends and family were affected by this traumatic event, and my colleagues needed to take over some of my teaching. I had to give up some of my Ph.D. students as well.

My shrink intervened. He'd also read Taleb. He said that in the follow-up to *The Black Swan*, *Antifragile*, Taleb introduces an idea that is the opposite of post-traumatic stress syndrome: post-traumatic growth, 'by which people harmed by a past event surpass themselves'. People who are suddenly disabled will over-compensate in order to achieve the same degree of success but in reality their efforts overshoot their goals by far. 'The excess energy released from overreaction to setbacks is what innovates!' Taleb writes. It made sense to me. My desire to travel and expand my memory project were certainly acts of over-compensation, attempts to make sure that my career and my future were not harmed by my stroke. But still, I thought, should I listen to my youthful self, like he said, and 'be at one' again? How could I do that?

Small explosions were going off in my head. 'Maybe I should take it slower, perhaps return to Amsterdam, a city with a slower pace compared to London, a more liveable environment?' I wondered. I was pretty distrustful of the slow movement, and the mindfulness zen yoga self-help rhetoric, but I thought I should be coming round to it. After my stroke, I loved the slowness that had been thrust upon me at first. I had experienced the three days in the French hospital as a kind of Eden; a sanatorium. I had returned to an innocent state, reset, an Adam reborn.

My psychologist nodded, said that such a move might be good for me. Retrenching for a while. Perhaps… But he was sceptical. 'You're a restless man, so a bit of change is good for you. You could embrace this new slowness as the basis for a new sensibility and lifestyle, at least for a while. But will retrenching really be a solution, Bas? It'll be a step back, and that just doesn't sound like you. It's not in your character. Maybe you should try the overcompensation route, which it sounds like you're on already. See where that takes you?'

Chapter Fourteen
A Wound without Pain

'Why do we pretend people around us do not exist when the only thing we're doing is to turn ourselves into ghosts?' I ask myself as I sit on the New York subway, on my way to Columbia University, where I'm about to attend a seminar on memory. It's a cliché of modernity, which I know all too well as a lonely Londoner. Right now, I'm surrounded by hundreds of Americans, rocked back and forth by the sway of the subway, but there's hardly any communication, not even a flash of eye contact, just people pretending to stare emptily into space, listening to 'their' music. This strange lack of acknowledgement of other people's existence bothers me. I want to connect.

It's February, six months after my stroke. I have flown to the East Coast of the United States to visit a group of colleagues specialising in memory; I hope to network with academics in various universities, try to set up an exchange programme between my own university and the University of Maryland in Washington; I will deliver a paper on surveillance at Yale University in New Haven; and I've got an appointment with one of the most famous neuroscientists working on memory, Suzanne Corkin, at MIT in Boston. All of this in the space of two weeks. I'm asking a lot of myself during what is supposed to be a period of recovery from a major brain infarct.

I get off the subway in West Harlem in the north of

Manhattan and walk to Columbia University for the symposium on memory. The snow throws back the low winter sun. The crisp lemon-yellow light illuminates the tenement buildings that have their fire escapes mounted to the front, a sight alarming because they remind one of possible disaster. I arrived yesterday and am jetlagged; I also have a slight pain in the left side of my brain near where the stroke happened. The ache in my head worries me even though there is a part of me that does not seem to care that much anymore: I have to live, enjoy myself, meet people. I'd rather choose human connection and die a few years sooner than live forever as a recluse. This is one thing I'm learning during my recovery.

I arrive at Columbia University's stately campus, have a cup of coffee and walk up to the seminar room where the symposium on memory is taking place. In the meeting, a group of French researchers outline how they used new eye-tracking technology – which measures people's eye-movement in order to analyse how their brains process the outside world – to create the best possible experience of a museum's exhibition on the Holocaust. The team discovered which photos, texts and objects were glossed over by the test subjects and which parts of the exhibition were of particular interest. In the end they even re-routed the exhibition to create a better experience for the audience.

Still tired after my flight, I decide to speak up. Our twenty-first-century minds are conditioned and reshaped by the strategic use of technology, I argue, and often for sinister purposes. Technology is so often deployed to make us do things, like buy stuff or vote for a political party. It's useful to understand how the brain processes the world around us, I say, but I also wonder what the role of *people* is in all this. Technology has become infinitely faster and smarter than the human brain. Is there a role for people here at all? The brain was now used to reveal secrets about our inner desires and turned against us – we're continuously being tricked. A heated debate about the ethics of technology ensues. I relish being back amongst like-minded colleagues.

On my way back from the seminar, my brain is set alight

by the discussion with my Columbia colleagues. I walk from Harlem through Central Park, from north to south. A professor of literature is accompanying me, our shoes sinking into the sparkling snow. I squint. Tiny shards of light bounce off the frozen water crystals. In the distance, skyscrapers stand out against the bluest of skies. New York, a living Cubist sculpture.

The literature prof is interested in my stroke and asks me about my experience, and how it's changed my perspective on language and literature – and life itself. I say that, because the stroke hit my language faculties so profoundly, I appreciate even more than before the importance of language as vital for a critical engagement with the world. I also have a more intense, loving relationship to language as the basis of meaningful connection between people – the level of intimacy depends on how intricately we use language. The more refined our language, the deeper our connection. I tell him that I make a conscious effort to expand my vocabulary, and use new words in my writing and chats to people. Whereas before I was always in a rush when writing emails or text messages, I try to be more careful in my communication. I don't just send stuff off the cuff but try to estimate how words and message will be interpreted by people, how they will be affected by my words.

Literature is the ultimate celebration of that linguistic bond between people, and between people and their understanding of the world. It's so strange to see that over the past decades the status of literature has been diminished. When I was studying literature in the 1990s and early 2000s, when a writer said something about a certain issue – like the collapse of Communism or 9/11 – people listened. A well thought-through and carefully expressed formulation of an insight or opinion still seemed to get at new truths. Those truths mattered and they shaped the world. By sidelining literature the whole world is experiencing some kind of collective stroke – a brain fog. But my belief in literature has only increased because of my stroke: I want to celebrate even more the connecting relationship that language forges between people and the world. In times like ours – with fake news eroding our democracies – we need literature more than ever. Literature is critical. My commitment has never been stronger.

He tells a story about Zora Neale Hurston, the incredibly prolific writer and filmmaker who wrote over fifty stories, essays and plays. From my studies I remember her being central to the Harlem Renaissance in the 1920s but her work was largely overlooked until Alice Walker, the writer who became famous for her 1982 novel *The Colour Purple*, put her back on the map in the mid-1970s. She was a pioneering anthropologist pursuing evidence for ethnic equality, researching society's habits and folkloric storytelling in Georgia and Florida, but also Jamaica, Haiti, and Honduras, which she reworked in her own fictional work as well as in auto-ethnographical collections with stories about hoodoo and black magic. In her late sixties, Hurston was substitute-teaching and moved on to writing journalism for the *Fort Pierce Chronicle*, though she started suffering medical troubles, including obesity, high blood pressure and an ulcer. In 1959, she suffered a stroke, leaving her weak and unable to concentrate, but she continued to live at home, where friends and neighbours spoon-fed her to keep her alive. After applying for welfare support for her medicines and food, she attempted to write, whenever she felt able, for the *Chronicle*. But she suffered another series of minor strokes, and entered St. Lucie County Welfare Home in Florida, where she died of heart failure.

The prof says that he believes she had already suffered a mini-stroke in 1958. Whereas her writing was always impeccable, she started making minor spelling mistakes: she wrote 'tyink' instead of 'think', 'og' instead of 'of' and 'adn' instead of 'and'. I tell him that I experienced exactly the same. In January 1959, just before suffering her stroke, she wrote one of her final letters to Harper Brothers publishers, trying to sell the book she was working on, a life of *Herod the Great*. The last line of if it goes: 'One reason I approach you is because you will realize that any publisher who offers a life of

Herod as it really was, and naturally different from the groundless legends which have been built up around his name has to have courage.' It's an extraordinary statement: it is not just about her myth-busting book but it is a testament to her own attitude to life.

It's about courage, I say to him. Writers are in the business of speaking the truth, of dismantling falsehoods that cloud our vision. Their task is complex and painful: to use imagination to make statements about real life. To conquer that pain you need courage. That's what *Don Quixote* is about.

Over the next few days in New York, I meet more people whom I invite to join my memory project. Every day I have breakfast at the same place, the Mayen Café in Midtown Manhattan, drinking fresh juice and eating bagels. In the evening, after my meetings, I order take-away meals, which I eat in my hotel room. It's all becoming very programmatic, I notice, too repetitive. I am also listening – listening only – to an album that I haven't heard for a long time, The National's *Alligator*. I listen to the tracks over and over again. What is going on with me?

On my final day in New York, I have an afternoon without meetings, and I take the subway to Williamsburg. Fresh snow has fallen generously on this pleasant 'village' this morning and my boots sink into the virgin whiteness. It's difficult to mark out the pedestrian paths and I'm zig-zagging my way down the dazzle. I get a jolt of recognition when I see Schermerhorn Street, a street deriving its name from a village just around the corner from where I grew up. There's a Flushing Avenue, referring to Vlissingen, a Hempstead, the New World version of Heemstede, and Brooklyn itself, referring to Breukelen. It's a strange linguistic remapping of two worlds, and languages: the Old and the New, on one level so completely different, but also deeply familiar.

I visit the Adam Yauch Park in Brooklyn, named after the rapper and bass player in the Beastie Boys who died of cancer. A mailman takes a picture of me in front of the entrance, and I send it to José. She responds saying she's jealous and wants to go to New York too.

A Wound without Pain

I say: 'With me?'

'Of course,' she replies. We text-chat for a bit, transporting ourselves back to our first date, nearly twenty years back. Afterwards I feel alone but also strangely intoxicated by the sensations that these affectionate memories of the Beastie Boys and the Brooklyn street names have aroused in me.

A couple of days later, after visiting colleagues in Washington D.C. to set up a student exchange between our universities, I'm on an Amtrack train to New Haven to the north of New York, finishing a funding proposal. Workwise there is a lot going on and I like it. I arrive in New Haven and check into my hotel, not far from the Yale University building where the conference on Surveillance in Twenty-First Century Culture is taking place.

The next day I deliver my talk at the Whitney Center for the Humanities: 'The eyes are the window to the brain: Contemporary Surveillance and the Synaptic View', an ironical adaptation of the Romantic idea that the eyes are the window onto the soul. I argue that the brain has become too central in contemporary culture; it's seemingly the only source of information about how people work. I caution against neurodeterminism and make a claim for the importance of culture, context and history as a means of understanding people. There is a danger in this new totalising scientific vision of society: the synaptic view, which believes that everything can be explained by analysing the neurons firing in our skull. A new kind of surveillance of human beings has emerged, taking place at the level of molecules and cells: this way of looking is no longer human, and can only be understood by neuroscientists who analyse data with algorithms. We are moving towards a new world order in which, as the literary critic Katherine Hayles argues, 'brain scans are no longer exotic procedures that most people will never encounter but the essence of what the future of humanity is envisioned to be'.

I'm aware that my take on the relationship between surveillance and brain technologies is far from subtle. Some of

169

the other delegates are challenging my argument. They say I'm exaggerating. It's an anti-neuromaniac's point of view. I do not tell them I've had a stroke but I realise my ordeal is influencing how I'm thinking about the importance of the brain in contemporary culture. My argument is contradictory: I am overstating the importance of the brain in culture because I've experienced first-hand how critical this organ is, but I'm also rejecting its significance because unconsciously this might be a way of moving on from my traumatic experience. My position is contradictory. I realise I need to find a way to reconcile my conflicting impulses. I need to move on, somehow, to transcend this stalemate position. But how?

When the conference has finished I'm tired and my brain happily hurts with the information it's been absorbing. It's been a while since I've concentrated so hard for an entire day. But it feels good, this type of exhaustion; I have missed it. At the conference dinner, I cannot help but confess that I'm recovering from a stroke and when I narrate Dickens' stroke story a Professor of Sociology tells me an anecdote about another stroke survivor. In 1919, President Woodrow Wilson collapsed in Pueblo, Colorado. Similar to Dickens, he was on a gruelling public speaking tour; he was trying to persuade the public to back the League of Nations, travelling by train and stopping frequently to make speeches. On returning to the White House to recover he suffered a second serious stroke in October, and this left him paralyzed on his left side and blind in his left eye. Wilson's condition was not only kept hidden from the public, but from members of the government too. A stroke is an embarrassment to the intellect and a potential threat to political power but, as I had experienced myself, it is not that hard to hide, if you're lucky.

When I walk back to the hotel, I tell myself that I enjoyed the conference and the dinner, and that I'm glad to be exhausted after spending a day amongst my colleagues. I'm reconnecting with and feel more comfortable around people.

So I am doing better but I am far from well. Every night in bed during my own tour of the East Coast I listen to 'The Geese of Beverly Road', a song by The National, four or five times in a row before I go to sleep. It's a melancholic song, and I can feel my mood dropping. I am worried about the neurotic patterns I am establishing. The album has become a kind of mantra; I imagine that my repetitive listening to The National's songs is like a secular form of counting rosary beads. This auditory compulsion is aimed at keeping control over my life and the world around me. I also understand that spending two weeks in hotels isn't helping me recover: the anonymity of the rooms is alienating me and it is heightening my sense of loneliness.

The next day, I'm on an Amtrack train taking me to Boston. When I get to the hotel, it turns out that my reservation has not come through. I'm cross about this, too angry, even I notice it; I should simply pay for the room and claim it back later, but I'm panicking, completely unnecessarily. The world outside my head is not conforming to my anticipation. This perceived lack of control, is it a sign that I'm no longer sure about my place in this world? Is a form of autism rearing up?

The MIT campus is a dream straight from a science fiction novel, a place with avenues lined with brand-new and brightly coloured buildings, and everywhere, even out on the streets, there's free wifi. It's a utopia of knowledge, and I love it.

I meet neuroscientist Suzanne Corkin and invite her to give a keynote at a conference I'm organizing in September. We chat for a bit about her work with the famous amnesiac patient Henry Molaison, set down in her book *Permanent Present Tense*, as well as about my stroke and its after-effects. Corkin tells me she likes my polka dot long-sleeve shirt; it reminds her of some sort of psychological test. I tell her I wasn't aware I was a walking personality experiment.

The trip to the States is a great success: I've recruited various new people for my memory project and I've managed to get colleagues from Yale, Maryland and MIT to support a new funding bid and come over to London for my conference. It's been a fruitful, productive time, despite my anxieties. I can relax, now.

On my last day, I go to Boston's Museum of Fine Arts and I stroll unsuspectingly into room 242. From all sides, familiar sights hit my eyes, producing a kaleidoscopic jumble of images: an ice skater, snowy landscapes, church spires, canal-side mansions, blue skyscapes, church naves. This maelstrom is making me giddy. I walk towards a painting depicting the Herengracht in Amsterdam, with its stately town houses overlooking the water that gives the light of Amsterdam its special, vibrant quality. There is also a painting of the Westerkerk by Jan van der Heyden, a church that I looked out on from my University of Amsterdam office. There is a painting of Haarlem, the interior of the St Bavo, the church where I went to pay respects to the priest who taught me Catholic catechism. Hendrick Avercamp's 'Winter Landscape with Skaters' depicts a hundred adults, kids and dogs having fun on the ice. A few guys are fishing through a *wak*, the Dutch word that translates not so beautifully as 'ice hole', others are using sleds and ice skating. The *wak* is symbolic: it's a warning that death lurks just beneath the surface of life. We should never neglect the soul, whose lightness allows us to escape death.

Nostalgia takes me over – I do not want it to, but it does – I have no control over it. For Dutchies, this is a very familiar sight. These paintings pull me back into the long history of my native country, and into my personal past. The images of sixteenth-century church spires, people ice skating, Amsterdam's canals: they're so familiar, they're in my blood, or, rather, in my brain. Memory is such a strange trick of the mind, and nostalgia is equally deceptive and alluring: a sentimental, false emotion. Why does nostalgia, this 'ache' for 'homecoming', exist? Reliving positive memories contributes to mental as well as physiological health: our body actually grows warmer when we contemplate fond memories. Nostalgia is a coping mechanism that helps your self-esteem and contributes to creating meaningful life. This is what these paintings are doing to me. It's a totally atavistic reaction, yearning for the safety of home in a place where I feel vulnerable.

A Wound without Pain

I leave the museum, walk along Huntington Avenue, the cold wind biting my face, but I hardly feel it: the new possibility plays in my head. A homecoming. No longer do I want to play The National. On Soundcloud I find my own band. I play our album *Cut Myself Shaving*, which we recorded in 1999, though it was never released because the record label started playing dodgy games. The disappointment was the final straw that made me decide to start a new life abroad. The first track – 'Stay' – starts. Guitars begin, the drums and bass are kicking in, the first verse opens, and before I know it the song is whipping me down the streets of Boston. I haven't listened to this album for a very long time; it feels fresh, as if the songs were written and performed by someone else – that younger me that's resurfaced. I like the vibe of this band, I genuinely do. To me the songs sound intelligent, slightly difficult but still poppy and catchy. Full on and loud as hell. I'd love to see these guys on stage!

So I continue to experience bouts of emotional dyscontrol and I don't know whether my emotions are genuine. But I see that I'm seeking out such specific experiences – I artificially create these circumstances. Even though this does not make them genuine, they seem to give me a degree of control. The obsession with my garden, the dream of organic growth and reintegration with nature and my pre-stoke self is completely artificial, I realise. No matter how well neuroplasticity is able to repair my brain, I am becoming a different man.

Chapter Fifteen
Prolonged Bleeding, Easy Bruising

It's still winter when I return to London but I'm more hopeful after my American trip and the discoveries I made there about myself. I'm longing for spring, for new life.

I visit my shrink, the familiar stranger whom I have allowed to poke around my life over the past six months, for one last time. I tell him about the insights that my trip to America has given me. That I have made a firm decision about how I want to live my life from now on. I need to be true to myself, I say, and follow my instincts, which are telling me that I must embrace my former younger selves and unite aspects such as innocence and sensitivity with all the fine things my life as an intellectual have given me: patience, attention to detail, understanding ambiguity. That is the way forward for me; by fusing the different versions of my personality I might arrive at my best self. It's a decision I've made with the utmost conviction.

He's glad at my reasoning. He wishes me well. He's here if I need a chat. His final piece of advice: 'I think you should pick up your guitar again. Play some old songs. Compose some new ones?'

Life continues, knowing I don't have my shrink to fall back on. I dust off my guitar. I speak with José every day now. My academic work proceeds, and so does my memory project. I have more meetings with the curators at the Whitechapel Gallery for our Chris Marker events. All speakers have been invited, plane tickets and accommodation have been booked. Everyone's excited. *A Cat Without a Grin* is the title of the exhibition.

In my spare moments I do more research into brain attacks and the effects on language. I learn that the wound in my head – the scar left behind by the injury to my brain's left anterior region – is called a 'lesion'. There is scar tissue inside my brain, a physical trace connected with psychical trauma. Freud states that brain injury is a wound without pain, which renders the presence of the injury questionable. If it doesn't hurt, it doesn't exist. Internal and thus invisible wounds affect us entirely differently than the external wounds that are intuitively familiar to us. We don't see internal brain wounds, so they escape our awareness. For me this isn't true at all. Although I know that many people do not experience pain during a brain attack, the headache during the first 48 hours after my stroke was very painful. I have a lucid memory of that dull, droning ache. The psychoanalyst was wrong to assume that aphasia comes with a painless wound.

Freud made this claim because there seems to be an opposition between external, visible wounds whose scar tissue we can touch and caress and the internal wounds inside the soft tissue of the brain. Freud was unable to see the scar tissue of people with brain injuries except via post-mortem autopsies. But for me, living in the twenty-first century, I have CAT scans and MRI images – a gallery of pictures to make an exhibition of my wound and the malfunctioning of my language, the source of my trauma, the Greek word for a physical wound.

External scars are significant because they enable you to point to, and/or symbolise, traces of the past; the evidence of events, incidents or accidents that left their mark on your body. You know the pleasure of rubbing a scar; it gives a sensory delight, even though the memories attached to it may not be pleasant. I myself have an inch-long scar on the palm of my right hand, which I got when I was four and fell on a shard of glass. When I rub this scar, I seem to console my former childhood self, retrospectively comforting and connecting with the boy who was resuscitated after my stroke. Though the original physical wound may have healed, the mental trauma may not have been resolved or have been worked through.

This is all the more complex for brain injuries or diseases of the ageing brain, like dementia, in which the wound is hidden inside your skull. Whenever I intuitively reach for my head, placing my hand over the area that was hit beneath my cranium, I caress the scar in my head. I nurse my wound to bring my pre-stroke persona back to life, mixed with a childhood version.

The act of nursing my internal wound gives me some respite, and perhaps a chance of somehow resolving via language this mysterious hiatus between the mind and body. My distorted language skills express and unite the pain of my internal wound as well as my damaged selfhood, my chaotic feelings. My misspelled emails formulate my wounds, past and present, and my broken mind. And my written gibberish confronts me, time and time again, with the reality of the violent brain attack itself, but also points to an uncertain future and the fact that the violence of the event is not yet known to me.

But language is the solution, I know. It is not only the measuring device of my internal being. Writing can help heal the physical wound and assist me in moving beyond my psychological trauma. Translating emotions into language, I have read, changes unmanageable feelings into more conscious forms that might allow me to tame the intensity of the chaos that sits inside me. But I was still not receiving therapy from the NHS and needed to figure out how to get better all by myself. Even so, I was getting more optimistic and my emotions seemed to have lost their extremes.

Time passed, and passed more and more quickly by the day, it seemed. It was March. Spring was here. Nature was awakening from its slumber on my study windowsill, where tomato plants and runner beans were growing in incubators. It was wonderful to see these tiny organisms grow; every time

I entered my study they seemed to be a little bit bigger and taller. They grew unstoppably, full of life. I'd developed an even greater connection with my plants and flowers because I seemed to hope, perhaps unconsciously, that their organic growth and regeneration was also happening inside my head.

Not that long ago, scientists discovered that it was possible to grow new brain cells. It was originally believed that once your cells had been generated in the first years of life, no more cells would be produced. This is not the case. The growth of new neurons helps prevent the impact of the ageing process on the brain and stimulates memory and enhances your mood. This is called neurogenesis, which can be enhanced by physical activity and learning. Physical exercise stimulates the generation of new nerve cells; a good workout or a session of football or any other sport can have a widespread effect on children's brains. The rate of production of new cells in the hippocampus is stimulated by antidepressants. Scientists now speak of 'long-distance migration of newly born neurons' that promote 'post-stroke neuroblast migration and behavioural recovery'. The rate of neurogenesis is detrimentally affected by ageing, stress and lack of sleep. We shouldn't overestimate the effects of this, though. We are not all of a sudden growing completely new cells, entirely new brains. But research did find neurogenesis and neural repair at the sites of stroke, which was promising.

During the weekends, I worked in my garden, preparing the transfer of the seedlings to the beds. Compost and fresh soil were waiting on the weeded beds. I'd tried imagining that my life was as it used to be, but every day there were signs or events reminding me of the stroke. When turning over the soil, I scraped the skin of my hand on a nail and the cut started to bleed. I sucked the wound clean, but the bleeding wasn't stopping. Normally a superficial cut would take a minute to stop bleeding, but now it took almost six, seven minutes. It was the Clopidogrel pills, the anti-coagulants I was taking, slowing down the healing process.

I also hurt the inside of my upper arm. A splotch of dark blood sat just below the skin, a slowly fading Rorschach test.

The medication leaflet confirmed the side effects of the meds: prolonged bleeding, easy bruising.

Physically I was feeling better: much less tired, and sleeping my normal eight hours, with plenty of dreams, some dark, some pleasant. Life was taking its course. Teaching was on track, and I was using recorded audio feedback to comment on my students' work. They actually preferred this to written feedback: the friendly voice of the lecturer seems less threatening compared to the violence of writing. I was seeing my friends in pubs and restaurants, going to concerts with them, and visiting art galleries. I ran again, about five miles on the Parkland Walk trail every other day; I no longer wanted to go to the gym to exercise; I saw it as too functional, too rational. As my desire for travel had showed me, I want to be out in the world – to connect.

At the end of April, I planted the seedlings in my garden. The runner beans soon snaked their way up. It helped me put at bay the neurotic behaviour I had displayed in the States – gardening gave me a sense of peace. But I'd been too rash, which was a sign that my pre-stroke character was coming back. A cold snap killed off the veg; their tiny lifeless corpses hung from the canes. I had run ahead of myself. I learned that I shouldn't rush things and try to trick my vegetables – and myself – into doing unnatural things, whatever they may be.

I noticed, though, that I was starting to get bored with living by myself. Living alone has many advantages, including farting without causing a domestic revolt, but I missed the intimacy of a close relationship, the deep, intimate contact. I longed for José but I wasn't admitting this openly to myself.

Our age is defined by the ambiguous myth of connectivity: we like, retweet and swipe ourselves through the many different lives we lead online, especially via social media, but also via dating websites and apps. We connect, but often it takes us away from ourselves and others – the screens and media are a barrier to meaningful relationships. Since the darkest days of emotional dyscontrol and sensory disturbances were now behind me, connecting with other human beings had become important. I felt a new urgency to get in touch with old friends I'd not seen in ages – in reality, to reconnect with nephews and nieces, to get my marriage back on track and to re-form my band.

I was fascinated by the ferocity of my renewed need for contact. I wanted to push the idea that all human thinking, action and memory is transactive, that is, a collectively shared networking activity between people and their machines – a gigantic global hive mind. Shared knowledge and memory were everywhere: they were the foundations of human existence. I call human beings 'prosthetic gods': we use technology, tools and other people to aid and extend our thinking and memory, and this allows us to become godlike, or at least to transcend our human limits. We aren't singular entities trapped inside our brains, but conceive of ourselves as being part of a network.

This was nothing new, of course. The very idea of society has sprung from the fact that we are creatures always looking for connection. Our need for socialising and romance are examples of interconnection, but the power of religion can partly be explained by the shared community that the church offers. Mourning also shows how human connectivity works. Losing a loved one can feel like an imagined amputation. Eight years ago, José and I lost her father to cancer. We were devastated; it was like feeling a limb being torn off. In the week after his death, I became scared of the dark – everything felt uncertain. Mourning is a deeply physiopsychological experience. People can literally die from a broken heart: bereaved people have a 41% higher risk of developing an irregular heartbeat.

A visit to my GP confirmed that my body was settling: my cholesterol was fine now, but my blood pressure was a cause for concern. It was consistently 150 over 100 whilst ideally it should be 130 over 80. The problem was that high blood pressure could make my blood push against the arteries too hard and cause another stroke. My GP threatened to put me on more medication. I needed to take care of my weight, cut my alcohol intake, and eat even less salt, even though I get enough exercise and have a healthy diet.

The doctor's orders made sense. But something else happened. I had arrived at a turning point. I admitted to myself that it wasn't my diet, level of exercise or salt intake that was wrong with my life but that I couldn't live without José. I missed her and our former life. We needed to be together. We both knew it. We'd both been miserable since we'd separated. We'd tried to learn to live without each other but it wasn't working. We were both lost. I finally had the courage to admit this truth to myself.

I took a train to Holland and asked José to meet me in Soundgarden, a bar in Amsterdam where we'd spent a lot of time when we first met. We sat out back in the beer garden overlooking the water, where swans were bobbing up and down the waves and canal boats with tourists cruised by. We engaged in some small talk. And then some more chitchat. I ordered another round. But then I couldn't contain myself any longer and said: 'José, I miss you. I miss you terribly. My life isn't working without you. And I think your life isn't either. We are soulmates. We can't not be together.'

She didn't say much, except for 'Yes, it's true. It's true.'

I suggested that we spend more time together, and that, if everything went okay, that we move back in with each other. We'd take things slowly. Her relief was just as big as mine. It wasn't the right decision – it was the only option. Us not being together was a lie, a denial. We embraced each other. We knew now that everything was going to be alright.

From that moment life sped up. I felt remarkably better. I devoted more and more time to writing my book on the sixties and continued to edit the collection of essays on memory with my colleagues. I spent longer on campus and had lunch with my co-workers. A new future was opening up – a life in which I could unite my softer self with a kinder literary critic. This possibility excited me.

In May, nine months after my stroke, José and I spent time together in our London garden, planting spinach, courgettes, pak choi and runner beans. We talked whilst working: it felt great to be planting vegetables together – to be so close again.

The next few weekends we spent together in Amsterdam.

The Whitechapel Art Gallery events were held during this time but colleagues covered for me. José and I had reached a tipping point and we needed to keep the momentum going for our relationship. For a while now, I'd not been working at the weekends; I was hanging out with friends and devoting time to my social life. My behaviour seemed altered. I wanted to have been changed.

Or did I? The trip to the States meant that high-profile neuroscientists, psychologists, philosophers and literary scholars had joined the Memory Network, and would attend a conference I was organising, and contribute to a book I would be editing. I had linked up my university with US counterparts with a view to setting up a student exchange programme. This achievement required a frantic schedule of meetings with dozens of people. The work had left me exhausted, but gratified.

More research into the history of the brain made me realise I was an 'unfortunate', at least according to one of the most successful guidebooks on the psychology of language. The author, Trevor Harley, wrote:

> The brain is very vulnerable to damage (which is why this precious organ is encased in a thick padded skull). Sites of damage to the brain are called lesions. Some unfortunate individuals suffer brain damage in a variety of ways, including strokes, brain surgery, and trauma from accidents (e.g. car crashes) or poisoning.

What did it mean to be an unfortunate? I wondered. The word derived from a negation of 'fortunate', which means 'lucky': I am un-lucky. 'Fortuna' was an interesting term for its complexity: in classical times it meant both 'chance' as well as 'fate', which are contradictory terms in the sense that the former means that something simply happens to you randomly, for no specific reason, whereas the latter assumes that the gods (or some kind of power) are in control, punishing you for evil deeds you may have committed against them – or there is something built into the fabric of your experience that you can't escape. It could be a character flaw, for instance – greed, ambition or uncontrollable lust – that brings you down. So, on the one hand, it indicates something accidental (an event over which you don't have control and for which you are not responsible), and, on the other, something you are responsible and thus culpable for – in which case your punishment is warranted.

In modern life, now that we no longer tend to believe in fate, things are even more complex. If there are no gods that control your life, either it is 'nature' or 'culture' or a combination of both that is responsible. Either I brought the stroke upon myself (through careerism, stress, too much *joie de vivre*, etc.), or I perhaps had some blood, heart, gene or brain condition that caused the stroke. This is why I had to discover the aetiology of my stroke because, if there was a clear cause, I would not be unlucky. If it was completely random, though, I was very much an unfortunate. I fell into the latter category.

Harley's use of the word 'unfortunate' brought me back to an experimental writer from the sixties, B. S. Johnson, on whom I was writing for a new book about sixties literature. One of his novels, *The Unfortunates*, comes in a box that contains 27 loose, disconnected chapters, which chronicle his memories of a friend who had died of cancer. Although the beginning and final chapters are fixed, the reader can read the other chapters in any random order. This means that the novel can be read in 15,511,210,043,330,985,984,000,000 different ways – millions of labyrinthine stories determined by chance. The reader re-orders Johnson's memories with every new reading. The experiment anticipates the lateral way we use the internet today, clicking from one website to the other, often quite randomly.

I suspected that *The Unfortunates* was winking at Dr Samuel Johnson's *A Dictionary of the English Language*, published over two centuries earlier. Although this dictionary contains endless cross-references and creates a web of interdependent meanings, a dictionary is first and foremost a linear ordering of the meaning of words that have been arranged in alphabetical order. B. S. Johnson's experiments had escaped the tyranny of linearity which he associated with the physical book. In a 1971 TV documentary on Dr Johnson, B. S. Johnson distinguished between maniacal writers and writers who need either a carrot or a stick to force them to write:

> There are some who are compulsive writers, who write against the odds. There are others, and [Samuel] Johnson was one, who write only when something forces them to. Dr Johnson needed a deadline, and fought a tendency against indolence and procrastination, besides a deep-seated melancholia and all his physical defects.

Though it wasn't exact science, I had learned from my collection of writers who survived strokes that this compulsive lot was the group particularly at risk of brain attacks. Looking at my own list of publications, I understood I had to include myself with the compulsive lot. Every day I had the urge to write. No one needed to tell me to put pen to paper.

In the documentary, B. S. Johnson was pointing to the catalogue of health problems Dr Johnson suffered throughout his life. Poor eyesight since childhood, lymph nodes in the neck (known at that time as the 'King's Evil'), depression, Tourette's Syndrome and gout were just some of the maladies he suffered, but a fear of going insane plagued him also. I investigated Johnson's maladies further.

In June 1783, Johnson had a stroke resulting from poor circulation, and he wrote to his neighbour, Edmund Allen, that he had lost the ability to speak. Two doctors were brought in to tend to him; he regained his ability to speak two days later. Heberden's *Index Historiae Morborum* notes: 'Voice suddenly went in man aged 74, mind and limbs affected; voice almost restored within a few days.' I was not unfamiliar with Johnson's loss of voice, though I was half his age when my stroke hit.

In a book on his illnesses, I found a quotation from a letter written by Johnson three days after his stroke:

I went to bed, and in a short time waked and sat up as had been long my custom, when I felt a confusion and indistinctness in my head which lasted, I suppose about half a minute; I was alarmed and prayed God, that however he might afflict my body he would spare my understanding. This prayer, that I might try the integrity of my faculties I made in Latin verse. The lines were not very good, but I knew them not to be very good, I made them easily, and concluded to myself to be unimpaired in my faculties.

Soon after I perceived that I had suffered a paralytic stroke, and that my Speech was taken from me. I had no pain, and so little dejection in this dreadful state that I wondered at my own apathy, and considered that perhaps death itself when it would come, would excite less horror than seems now to attend it.

In order to rouse the vocal organs I took two drams. Wine has been celebrated for the production of eloquence; I put myself into violent motion, and, I think, repeated it. But all was in vain; I then went to bed, and, strange as it may seem, I think, slept.

The book's author commented on how the stroke's consequences manifest themselves in Johnson's letter: 'the manuscript shows an unusual number of insertions and substitutions. For example, the word "body" was first omitted and inserted later.' Some lines were mangled originally: 'This prayer that I might the integrity of my faculties I made in Latin verse. The lines were not very good but I know not to be very good.' Johnson corrected them retrospectively. He confessed: 'My hand, I knew not why, made wrong letters.' Dr Johnson's critic states: 'Johnson's was not only a disorder of speech but a "dysgraphic" one, in which patients have difficulty expressing themselves in writing: a true aphasia, the loss of the faculty of language.'

In the eighteenth century, the medical world was less advanced; people, including doctors, still believed in the four humours of Hippocratic medicine – black bile, yellow bile, phlegm and blood. To cure the stroke, Johnson thought that a vigorous and rough vomiting would help 'rouse the organs of speech to action'. Doctors put a salve that made the skin blister on his back and on his throat to provoke his speech to return. Johnson recovered quite quickly, but obviously not thanks to this treatment.

Chapter Sixteen
Information Overload

It's a hot, clammy summer, which I spend harvesting vegetables in the garden. Often José is with me in London but for most of the time I have been with her in Amsterdam, also reconnecting with old friends and spending more time with my family. I am consciously making more space for people, engaging in long, deep talks. This is new version of me, caring, more empathetic.

My academic life is in another gear as well. I am preparing a one-hour long keynote speech on information overload at a prestigious conference in Edinburgh. I've been reading up on systems theory, physics, neuroscience, as well as fiction and poetry, from T. S. Eliot's poetry to Dave Eggers' dystopian novel, *The Circle*. I've put an extraordinary amount of effort into this talk.

At the end of the summer, I'm in Scotland. I'm anxious. It's the first big talk since my stroke. Will my brain be able to keep up? Will I glitch? I think of the talk as a litmus test – an assessment that will determine if my academic life is back on track. Once I have given the talk, I will need to go back immediately to London, as my own memory conference – *The Story of Memory* – is starting. I have taken on a lot, perhaps too much. Ironically, I'm overloading myself, but I want to show to my colleagues that I'm back, that my brain and body are fit and ready to take on new, big tasks. That I'm my old, busy self again. I'm performing – overperforming – my old self. Have I learned nothing?

Information Overload

The keynote goes well. I'm over-prepared: I've timed the talk to perfection, the audience is engaged, and I receive good questions. During my talk I use neuroscience to show that the mind is under attack by new technologies. A debate ensues about the ways in which we must safeguard the human mind and avoid addiction.

At the follow-up workshop, we focus on the importance of the brain. In the world of the humanities, there is huge interest in the brain. Scholars are fascinated by this organ and there is a lot of unspoken envy for the knowledge that contemporary neuroscientists are generating. There are some neuroscientists who want to understand writers, and the act of creation, and creativity, by measuring the brain's activity during writing. A team of neuroscientists used electroencephalography (EEG) to measure the brain of the Dutch writer Arnon Grunberg, who was wired up for two weeks. Except for a lot of media attention, the resulting data yielded nothing of note. Yet it feels that neuroscience is encroaching onto the territory of the Humanities. Despite my stroke, which demonstrated the power of the brain in my experience, I'm becoming increasingly resistant to neuromania. Language, art and culture are being sidelined and I see we're in danger of limiting our vision on the world to just scientific perspectives. We must stop this. We must bring together the arts, humanities and the sciences, as I'm arguing in my book on memory.

Before I know it, I'm on a train taking me back towards my own conference on memory, which is in full swing when I arrive. Suzanna Corkin, the neuroscientist I met at MIT in the States during the winter, is delivering her keynote. Other talks about the state of memory are given by speakers from around the world, including the Yale Professor of Psychology, Paul Bloom. Ideas and theories are whizzing by, and everyone seems happy about the new ground we're breaking. We end the proceedings with a literary festival on memory with Ian McEwan and Naomi Alderman. We end the conference with a dinner at a St Pancras pub. I'm tired but contented. My keynote talk and the conference have been excellent. I seems I have re-established my role as an academic. On the tube back home, I feel happy. 'I'm back,' I think. Yet, looking at my distorted reflection in the carriage window, a question pops into my head. 'Yes, I'm back alright. But is that a good thing?'

Next to my academic renaissance and practising my language skills, I try to regain my confidence in different ways. I organise band practice for the first time in nearly ten years. We have a reunion gig lined up in an underground bar near my birthplace. I want to take revenge on my stroke for having had to cancel my fortieth birthday gig.

During the beer breaks, stories keep emerging, mostly memories about broken band buses. The one about the lead guitarist driving our rented van into a height restriction barrier when we played on the beach at Scheveningen. And about our band bus being broken into, but our gear remaining miraculously untouched – the thieves wanted the Mercedes, not the amps and guitars. And of our own Volkswagen van, proudly acquired with money we'd saved from our gigs, breaking down in the middle of the motorway just a week after we'd bought it.

Singing proves remarkably difficult – I am hoarse after an hour – but it's wonderful at the same time. We are a bit rusty at first, but some kind of sonic memory kicks in: the music triggers the lyrics which emerge from my mouth as if I wrote them yesterday. After tentatively finding the chords on the guitar and the drummer reminding himself of the ridiculously difficult breaks we'd invented, the songs simply emerge – intact, fresh.

The day after the rehearsal, I wake up feeling different. I've experienced a series of very clear dreams from episodes of my life. José and our first holiday together in California and Mexico in 1995; graduating in Amsterdam; lots of band stuff. My mind continues to be very vivid during the day, as if the lucidity of the dreams continues to infect my perception. I imagine I can hear the blood travel through the capillaries in my brain, in places that were shut off before. I send the guys a message:

Guys, there is neuroscientific evidence that listening to (live) classical music activates most parts of your brain (much more so than pop music and certainly more than watching television). There is also research that suggests that singing is very good for people who have suffered strokes. Yesterday I experienced both. I had wild, hyper-real dreams and feel incredibly lucid this morning. Like my mind has been opened up. Marvellous. Thank you, gentlemen. Until soon.

After each band practice I wake up with my mind blown open. When I run or go to the gym, the adrenalin makes my entire body feel alive and sharp, but singing really hits me right in the head. Singing, I mean, real singing, in which you need to belt out lyrics to compete with a band's amplified instruments, is hard. The nature of the strain you have to put on your entire body to sing the notes creates pressure on your vocal cords, throat, your chest, belly and your head. Your breathing changes, and your body ensures all energy is aimed at your head, where your mouth releases seemingly invisible streams of air that resonate with the other sonic turbulence in the room.

There is another development. I receive an email from a student therapist working for the Speech and Language Therapy department of my local hospital. This was the moment I had been waiting for: the NHS reaching out to me to help my recovery. I speak with her on the phone and, although it's been a long time since the actual stroke event, we decide to meet up for an assessment. I need to bring my MRI scans, neurologists' letters and sample writings.

She's in training and not yet properly qualified but I tell her I'm very happy to finally to see someone. A week later we meet in a depressing 1970s building, with leakage stains on the ceiling, paint scaling off. But I like my therapist: she's engaging, interested in my writing, and my personal story and background. She looks at the MRI scans of my brain, and sees the white cloud where the stroke hit. Luckily I had my stroke in France, I tell her, and was admitted to a specialist neurological unit. The care I received there was excellent; I felt very safe, despite the horrible event inside my head. The aftercare in the UK was wanting: at every step of the way there was chaos, or no help whatsoever. I never expected this level of health care in a supposedly first-world country. She drops a bombshell: 'The UK is the worst place for having a stroke in Europe. It is time we rethink the NHS.' I'm shocked by this frank admission but then again I'm not surprised. She continues: 'I'd rather pay health insurance that provides excellent healthcare and reduces waiting lists than receive so-called "free" treatment that is stressfully chaotic and puts lives in danger.'

I nod and say that it's not that easy to change the system, that it will take time – or just a much bigger government investment. A large part of the population will not be able to afford health insurance. 'The entire socio-economic system in the UK is geared against the working classes,' I say. We're both silent.

We leave politics aside and look at my situation. I tell her my concerns: the deterioration of my writing since my stroke and subsequent aphasia, and the problem of being a non-native English speaker. She empathises. I tell her that I've lost confidence in my performance as an English literature lecturer: I avoid speaking in front of colleagues and need to take extra care when I'm writing emails, but still I make mistakes. Is there any way I can be helped?

We move to an assessment of my spelling, which requires me to single out the correct version of a given word. I do the test, with twenty words, and get one wrong: 'pronunciation', which I always think of as 'pronounciation' as in 'to pronounce'. The rest are pretty easy: I have made mnemonics for potentially difficult words such as 'occurrence' or 'necessary' – only double 's'; 'millennium' – both double consonants. 'Separate' is easy as it's a conjunction containing 'apart', that is, not joined together. 'Liaison' is easy as the other two options weren't spelled with 'iai' – the 'a' sandwiched in between the i-i. She says that this is not bad at all, although she figures that an English Literature lecturer should not have any problems with the spelling of higher-level words. Her verdict makes me feel ashamed, a bit.

She writes down on a sheet of paper:

Strategies
Slow down!
- Be a CONTENT editor: think about the meaning of words
- Be a COPY editor: proofing

She suggests I buy a book, *Advanced Grammar in Use*, which contains tests. I could also train myself to write plain English, for instance by looking at a *New York Times* website on editing. She also has other ideas for therapy: voice recognition software, text prediction software, grammatical tests with explanations and TEFL-style grammar exercises. This will help me get my language abilities back in shape, or, at least, cover up the mistakes that I'm making. Otherwise, there isn't much we can do. I just have to practise more, and rebuild the spelling and grammatical structures in my brain.

I see her two more times. We talk about how strokes affect bilinguals like me. When the brain is young, there is still an overlap between the brain areas that process words and visual information. In the mature brain, specialisation has taken place so that you learn a new language (called 'L2' – language 2) with your 'L1'-brain, which is the language of your immediate environment, usually your home country, but also the accent of your local or regional environment. This happens in a different sub-area, and not the original area. Your environment creates permanent changes in your brain structure and function. If you learn a second (or third) language when you are a child, however, there is no distinction between L1 and L2 as both are processed by the same area. They are produced simultaneously rather than sequentially.

When you move from speaking in L1 to L2, or vice versa, this is called code-switching. There is much research into the costs and benefits of code-switching, and the jury is out when it comes to negative effects of bilingualism: it seems there is a

191

slight deficit in the cognitive processing of the second language, that is, being bilingual costs the brain more energy to perform the second language – 'increasing proficiency in L2 by immigrant children is associated with reduced speed of access to L1', though other researchers have argued that 'there is no obvious processing cost attached to being bilingual'.

But – and now it gets interesting – there is a 'gain in metalinguistic awareness, cognitive flexibility, and superior verbal fluency'. Researchers have shown that children in the Canadian immersion program (for learning French) tended to score higher on tests of creativity than monolinguals. Bilingual children, compared with monolingual children, show an advantage in knowing that a word is an arbitrary name for something. In this sense, bilinguals are all post-structuralists: post-structuralism was a hip theory in the latter part of the twentieth century that acknowledged not only that we need to make a distinction between the objects and events in the world and the language which we use to describe them, but that we need to understand that the words that we use to describe the world are completely random. There is no intrinsic reason that a cat, the animal, is called 'cat' and not 'dog' or 'Volvo'. If we all decided to call cats 'Volvos' that would be no problem. The point is that if you are keenly aware that the language we use to think and communicate is a separate system built on chance, you are more aware of the internal politics and biases of that system.

What is even more interesting is the fact that bilingualism confers a general cognitive advantage in the form of enhanced flexibility. There is even evidence that being bilingual protects people to some extent against developing Alzheimer's disease by helping to build up the mind's 'cognitive reserve' that slows down cognitive ageing. It seems interesting to me that some of the most interesting modern writers were not only bi- or trilingual, but also write in their L2 or even L3 language: Joseph Conrad, Franz Kafka, Samuel Beckett, William Gerhardie and Vladimir Nabokov all wrote in the language they acquired at a later age. Conrad wrote in his third language: his 'linguistic variety conveys a diversity of cultural viewpoints accounting for his status as a cosmopolitan writer'. Nabokov's verbosity and wit demonstrate his superior verbal fluency and his status as a truly international writer. It seems to me that these transnational writers and their cultural and linguistic miscellany contributed to a spirit of openness and tolerance that we in the twenty-first century could embrace more. Their writing points towards a world without borders.

In our final session, we do some more tests and practice. I make a few mistakes, but not many – and my performance is actually very strong, which is not surprising, given my Ph.D. in English Literature. I thank my therapist for her efforts with me. In her Discharge Summary, she writes: 'Dr Groes seemed concerned about his performance at work and keen to regain his confidence. On assessment, he showed no signs of difficulty with receptive language, but demonstrated some high-level words finding and writing difficulties. He agreed to work towards a goal of increasing his confidence in language tasks at work.'

That is all. Class dismissed. I had something else to turn my attention to: my band's European tour was about to kick off.

Chapter Seventeen
Sing for Life

People are pogoing in a circle pit, pushing and shoving. Shouting. Applause. I'm treated to a beer shower. The room is roaring with joy and the cacophony of banter and laughter. I'm ripping my vocal cords out, tearing myself through lyrics that are imprinted in my memory. *We're strolling through this earthly maze, lost souls trapped in this rat-race.* The lines written by my younger self, a teenager angry at worldly injustices caused by capitalism. People are singing along. A hot stinging sensation nestles itself at my skull's base. *I see those dollar signs in your empty eyes, I feel your greedy hands pulling me down.* My brain fires away in ecstasy and delighted by the beauty of this lovely filthy mess. The Fiddler's Elbow in Camden has turned into a loud, sweaty rock'n'roll joint crammed with elated music lovers.

We are finishing our self-organised, far-from-grand-but-totally-awesome European tour with a 40-minute set of our high-speed bitter-sweet in-your-face punk rock. We played in Hamburg, Amsterdam, the Dutch naval town Den Helder, and we are finishing in London. This final gig feels like the end of a chapter in my life because it also seems the end of my stroke journey. I'm finally playing the gigs that had to be postponed because of my brain infarct.

We've been on the road for a week and saying goodbye to German band members and other tour buddies is more difficult than we imagined. We're already nostalgic for the intoxicating times we've shared these past seven days. My lead guitarist, shirt covered in beer, lays his head on my American friend's shoulder, his face tired and sad. We have found true camaraderie, and I have been able to restore relationships with friends I'd lost along the way. And I've made some new friends, for life.

At home, we drink more beer and whisky whilst our drummer flips burgers. At two o'clock in the morning I decide it's time for an impromptu symposium on our favourite Beatles tracks. My drummer argues for 'A Day in the Life' because it shows why Lennon and McCartney complement one another so well, and because it's an experimental song with lots of ideas from George Martin. My guitarist opts for 'Piggies', a curious choice, questioned by everyone, but, intoxicated, he states that it's the best song to combine a profound meditation on the animal kingdom with absolutely mediocre song writing. José chooses 'Glass Onion' because it cleverly incorporates lots of references to other Beatles songs. The guitarist changes his mind, withdraws 'Piggies' and argues for *Abbey Road*'s B-side medley after 'Golden Slumbers' because they're really one single song and the best pieces ever recorded: excellent composition, fantastic melodies, sublimely executed. The lead guitarist likes this argument, but he chooses 'For No One', because of the seemingly playful way in which Lennon conjures up the song's brilliant melody. My favourite is 'Happiness is a Warm Gun', because it's such a diverse song, with a surreal title, and the way Lennon's breaking voice rips through the final lyrics just kills me.

On the balcony, I inhale the warm summer air, enjoying the atmospheric texture that only London has – a confused, confusing concoction of grimy anger and toil never far below the elusive promise of hope. I look out onto the street where I have lived for over eight years, and that I know so well: the houses, the street, and Priory Park, an extension of myself.

We're moving to Seven Sisters, just two miles east, but a different world that still feels real, authentic. By moving east, I need to look at my city from a different angle: I need to tilt the compass in my skull ninety degrees. I'm deliberately scrambling my inner compass: my brain will need to adapt, mutate, and rewire itself.

An antique book with a history of London place names that I acquired in a Hampstead bookstore now long gone gives a fascinating etymology for the name Seven Sisters:

> Said to have been named from seven trees which were planted by seven sisters, one of them a cripple. Of the trees, six are supposed to have grown straight and the seventh to have been deformed, it having been planted by the cripple.

Still feeling slightly disabled and vulnerable myself, I feel for that sister, and I imagine she'll help me start a new chapter.

On a certain level I have started to embrace my stroke as a strange blessing. I have begun to accept the trauma caused by my stroke and the neural reorganisation in the aftermath. It has given me a third reminiscence bump: the intensity of the experience and my recovery laid down a series of densely clustered memories, epiphanies and insights. All those discoveries seemed to have been burnt into my brain with a branding iron. The force of the experience has allowed me to embark on a new path.

I am all the more determined to unite my vision of art and literature with my knowledge of the sciences. My memory book is nearly done; it's become a defence of the importance of the arts and humanities in society. Though I cannot deny the importance of the brain, this doesn't mean that science is the only means to understand life. Science exists within our shared human culture. A writer said it for me when he wrote to me in an email:

> We don't think in our brains alone: we think in language, and history, and culture. If you want to understand mental life, you don't slice up a murderer's, cabbie's, or even Will Self's brain: you read *Antigone*, and *Macbeth*, and watch David Lynch's films. This is the fundamental, radical

proposition of the arts, and always has been, and it's had to fend off reactionary attempts to close it down and stamp out its subversive play of symbolic movement with an absolute transcendent meaning, be this God or the author's supposed 'message' – or now, most recently, some ultra-reductive positivism in the form of neuroscience. MRI scanning Shakespeare won't explain *Hamlet.*

When I hear 'What is the neural basis for this?' I cringe at this reductive question. Our bodies and other people are connected on various levels with our mental life. The idea that the brain determines everything is dangerous because of its closed-mindedness: just as with eugenics a century ago, this one-dimensional attitude could lead to a new kind of radicalism in which much of life is determined by attention to the brain and by the brain alone.

My stroke has also given me a new understanding of art and culture. Art does not happen on the page, on the stage or screen, nor is it an object like a painting or sculpture, but it's a process that happens when people's brains, bodies and minds are drawn into a thinking loop with the work of art, its aesthetic triggering felt reactions, some of which can be verbalised and rationalised whilst other responses cannot. Sensations engendered by the art experience come before words and are partly non-conscious. This is why the Enlightenment as an approach to knowledge and, speaking more generally, as a lifestyle, failed: it mistook rationality for wisdom, and excluded the non-conscious side of the human mind, which is erratic, fickle and contradictory. This is why neuromania is dangerous. Ultimately, we must accept that, even though we know a lot about the brain, the mind remains a self-jesting mystery: it wants to understand itself but cannot.

My stroke threw my brain off balance and showed me its importance in thinking, in my emotional life, my sensory perception, and my ability to communicate. The stroke's effect was not unlike the best of art. It is art's job to make our shared boring, automatized reality strange through artistic devices and in particular *poetic* language because it breaks down ordinary speech and thereby also thinking. Routine, automatic behaviour ensures that we can no longer see the world for what it truly is – a strange marble that temporarily houses animals with highly developed cognitive abillities floating through space. My stroke has taught me exactly what artists across many centuries had achieved: to effect defamiliarization, hitting the brain to make it come alive, inviting it to reset and rethink one's relation to the world.

Just as my band has done just now: ripping through everyday reality. I look through the window and see José and my bandmates sitting around the dining room table, bathed in pale light – drinking, talking, eating, laughing. I'm so lucky to be part of this union between myself, my biggest love and this band in my home – the connection is disarming, humbling. I'm filled with love for them, and, although I want to tell them this, I know that saying it aloud would spoil it.

Looking through the glass I see an image of what human beings truly are. We are taught to think of ourselves as distinct from others, as unique selves; it is easy to love and be committed to one single person fully; it is much more difficult to care for a large group of people. People who embrace themselves as individuals as opposed to thinking of themselves as part of a network have better defined goals in life and achieve targets more easily; they are also, on the whole, much happier. But, whilst looking at my friends through the window, united in laughter and chatter, I see we are connected by invisible strings, a shared collective of minds whose brains fire together, perhaps not always in harmony, but connected nonetheless.

The human brain has become as large as it is because we are social animals. Grooming and physical contact release growth hormones in the brain: caressing, tickling, sex have a positive effect too. Fact: loneliness reduces growth of the brain and has a detrimental effect on your health. As an experimental psychologist says, 'without the love of others, we are lost as individuals, unable to form the social behaviours that are so necessary to becoming a normal social animal'.

And then I know: I'm not an unfortunate. I am fortunate: I survived my stroke. Also, I have learned and discovered. I have changed and become a different – a better person: more patient, more empathetic.

I'm not the first stroke survivor to say that it's love that drives the world. Yet this is exactly what my brain attack has taught me: I must continue to acknowledge the force that gives our shared human world hope: love, kindness, compassion, humility, generosity and self-sacrifice are the qualities we need to survive as human beings; they will be able to help us imagine new ways of being human whilst helping us to navigate the paths that lead to our shared future, which at the moment seems increasingly fragile and uncertain.

'Only connect,' said E. M. Forster over a century ago, and we must repeat his words again today and build bridges between the different groups that are no longer talking to one another. Humanity as a network across space and time, as a matrix of creative possibilities, ready to work together against the series of dark, global crises we are facing, from the climate crisis to humans being replaced by Artificial Intelligence. Together we are stronger than the destructive, deceptive illusion of individualism. We are an army of ants. We are a festival. We are schools of fish shoaling; a swarming multitude – a pack of wolves. We are a flock of birds, a murmuration of starlings, the beautiful transformation of tiny individual starlings connected in a graceful aerial ballet, turning, twisting, changing constantly – together one.

And, at that moment, out on the balcony, I mark this point in time as the end, as a start: I have completed my odyssey of discovery and learning. I see the task that lies before me. After the loss of my speech and ability to write, after the disturbances and dyscontrol, after my depression and manic episodes, I understand it is my task to write and teach, to help forge and foster the shared, collective experience that makes up this world. To explain the urgency of art and culture, and the importance of human language and communication for our relationships, and to show the value of being able to express yourself in a refined and subtle manner, truthful and distinctive, preferably without cliché. It is time to immerse myself in the swaying, swirling, seasick ocean that is humanity.

Epilogue

Looking back, four years after completing the first version of this story, and then seven years after subsequent revisions – the book has changed substantially, though its essence has stayed the same over the years. The book's artificially crafted trajectory in the final part surprises me. It was, it now seems to me, written by someone else, an earlier version of me, deeply impacted by the mental consequences of the stroke. The performed optimism of the euphoric ending (perhaps another influence by Joyce, this time *Ulysses*), where I *willed* to make my life turn out alright, seems to obscure a much less rose-coloured journey. The feel-good story that I had created seems to obfuscate a more sober, pedestrian story that would have been truer to reality and perhaps more informative and useful – but perhaps less appealing to the reader.

The organic drive that I factitiously used as a mould for the outcome now reads to me as contrived (even though those trips and the band tour happened). Casting the story as an 'epic existential journey' was the result of a retrospective sense-making process. I see now that the trauma was very deep: I wasn't in control of my world and the stroke was just another affirmation of that. Rather than concede this fact, I (perhaps unconsciously) chose to put the story on a different track that led to a classic fictional reshaping. A tragedy that backed out, transforming itself into climactic, orgiastic drama with a happy ending.

This life-affirming attempt at restoring my former identity

in this contrived trajectory rubs up against the fact that the connection between narrative and identity is bogus in the first place. Did I really think I could make myself better by writing a neat, euphoric conclusion? Although I mention the mismatch between story and self on various occasions, the trajectory of the narrative betrays my attempt to overthrow both the neuromaniacs and the misbegotten intellectuals whose mantra about the self being an illusion was hip for a brief period, as well as those who believe in the simplistic idea that the self is a story. I do believe there is a character, and I also believe there is a self (complex, refracted, many aspects of it unknown but still *there*, somehow), yet what this book wants to demonstrate, and which it should have stressed more adamantly, is that within the experience of life there is much less control than we think over who we are, how we live, how much positive power we have in shaping our lives. The stroke was, if anything, a metaphor for this fact: the blatant, undeniable rough power of the experiences that we do not control but that determine our lives.

So, I wavered and recoiled, then retrenched into artifice. I needed fiction as a coping mechanism. The recovery never came full circle, neatly, organically with a clear cutting-off point. There was never a heroic return.

But perhaps the distorted, evasive form of this book itself says something about how difficult it is for those with (brain) trauma to come to terms with the hardness and the darkness of implications of the truths with which they – we – are confronted. Perhaps readers will see this as another hedging move, a cop out, but my doubts about the book's orbit can to a degree justify the lyrical, romanticised ending.

There is another layer that explains why I fled towards the artificial construction of this story's finale. As the narrator has hinted in these pages on several occasions, he – I – understand my own life and the world best through the imagination. I seem more comfortable appreciating events, probably at my own peril, in fictional terms. My conversations with the psychologist who tried to help me cope with the mental impact of my stroke gave clear reasons why this might be so. (And, trust me, so many things have had to be left unsaid, for various reasons.) I also make my living understanding how fiction is a distorting mirror that makes us see the world more clearly. In fact I do not see the point of making a distinction between lived experience and imagined adventuring – both are extensions of each other, intentions thwarted by or struggling with external forces, desires, fantasies. Whether they're 'real' or not to me seems of little concern. They're all part of the cognitive looping journey that is human experience.

Looking back, what feels like years and years after the actual stroke event, I feel I must take the opportunity to provide a slightly more sober reflection on my post-stroke life. Despite the blissful ending, I haven't committed to the New Age movement, haven't become a hippie, and I'm still sceptical of the Slow Movement, I am not suddenly into the Lord, nor do I wake up everyday singing Hallelujahs, as the book's last chapter-ending might suggest. I have moved on in many ways: I moved jobs, moved to another city, and I've said goodbye to a younger self who experienced the ordeal described in this book. When I am tired, I still make mistakes in speech and writing – I have to admit that the stroke has and will have a lasting effect on my ability to express myself. I also continue to make hard decisions about what is important and what is less significant: although the first, sharp, strong rejections of any non-essential stuff in my life has worn off, I do still have a sense of urgency, of needing to cut out the less important stuff in my life.

What persists also is a lingering yet undeniable sense of gratitude for having survived, and for having been aided by my friends and family, who have helped me correct and steer my life into calmer waters. I have written the book for them – for showing me the power of my connection with them.

First and foremost, I made the book for my fellow stroke survivors and their carers, to show the major social and psychological impact a brain infarct can have. I wrote it because I wanted to capture the full force of being alive, of rediscovering life in all its majestic and multitudinous beauty. Being able to satisfy the need for human beings to connect, share and be part of a collective, a community – it is vital for our survival as individuals, but also for the planet, which is facing a future fraught with mindboggling problems. I believe that together we can handle them – if we are united in our purpose and resolve to safeguard humanity.

Acknowledgements

It's taken me a long, long time to finish *Right in the Head.* The book has gone through many iterations, and was guided by a number of different readers and editors, who all left their subtle yet important mark on the story: Adrian Mathews, my long-time friend whose careful editing shaped this book early on; Sean Matthews gave it an eagle-eyed proofing; Nick Lavery and Peter Harvey gave the story a sharp reading and Macdonald Daly's editorial incisiveness and unrelenting ability to cut through bullshit were similarly important. I need to thank Ian McEwan, Peter Straus and especially Matthew Turner at Rogers, Coleridge & White for their initial help with this book.

Un grand merci beaucoup to the staff at the neurology department at Albi Hospital in France, as well as the staff at the Queenswood Medical Practice, Speech and Language Therapy section, Haringey Health Services and the Royal Free Hospital, for putting up with such an impatient patient. I'd like to thank my colleagues in the English and Creative Writing Department at Roehampton University for covering for me in the immediate aftermath of the stroke event; Laura Peters, who was my line manager at the time, is especially thanked for her professional and sensitive handling of my recovery.

Members of the Memory Network, and Stefan Besser especially, also deserve thanks for helping me. Nick Lavery, my trusted editorial and writing partner and friend is thanked for continuing to stand by me. Adam Roberts put me onto the trail of Sir Walter Scott's and Charles Dickens' strokes –

thanks, Adam, you are a Genius. Will Self and Hugo Spiers collaborated with me on an important experiment in human spatial navigation; I am grateful to Barry C. Smith for his support; I thank Tom McCarthy for letting me quote from an email exchange; Wendy Moncur was an important supporting force in my life during the period after my stroke; and Asifa Majid, too, was an important sounding board at the time.

Right in the Head is full of quotations, paraphrases, memories of conversations, memories of memories as well as allusions to literature, music, film etc. The title of the final chapter is taken from my friend Douglas Cowie's *Sing for Life* novellas (Black Hill: 2013).

I thank Kathy Prendergast for letting me use her artwork – *Hippocampus* – which was commissioned by the Creative Intelligence Agency.

Corin Depper, James Machin and Tony Paraskeva and the Primavera gang are thanked for their friendship. And thank you, Jason Tougaw and David Driver, you two are awesome. Thank you to my Dutch music buddies Daan, Pieter, Christiaan, and Robert, Faisel Rajjab, and especially Wouter, who has been a friend for over twenty years and knows me like no other. Thanks to Andy, Al and David of Probably Your Teacher.

The stroke ordeal kind of got me back in touch with my old friend Rink again, as well as with Sander Foen-a-foe. I thank my parents, André and Ellen, for their support, as well as Sandra, Arjan, Tim and Lisa Lapré for their love and companionship. Our father, Otto, was a beacon in our life, and since his departure I guess we cannot help but feel a bit rudderless – but we'll make it through together. A very special Thank You goes out to my buddy Doug Cowie, who edited one of the first iterations of this book. We've travelled a long way, Doug, and I cannot thank you enough for being my friend and helping me through various trying situations.

Most of all I thank José Lapré with gratitude and humility for our shared life journey together.

B. G.
Wolverhampton/Amsterdam, 2023

List of Figures

Figure 1 MRI scans taken at Centre Hospitalier d'Albi

Figure 2 Wernicke's area

Figure 3 MRI scans taken at Centre Hospitalier d'Albi

Figure 4 Reminiscence bump

Figure 5 Kathy Prendergast, *Hippocampus*.

UK-based stroke organisations

The Stroke Association: www.stroke.co.uk.

Different Strokes, for younger stroke survivors: www.differentstrokes.co.uk.

The NHS has a website dedicated to stroke: https://www.nhs.uk/conditions/stroke/.

Useful beginner's guides to stroke

My Stroke Guide, a guide by the Stroke Association: https://www.stroke.org.uk/finding-support/my-stroke-guide.

Jonathan A. Edlow, *Stroke*. Westport, Connecticut and London: Greenwood Press, 2008.

John R. Marler, *Stroke for Dummies*. Hoboken: Wiley, 2011.

Life after Stroke, a guide by the American Stroke Association: https://www.stroke.org/en/life-after-stroke.

Stroke memoirs

Susannah Cahalan, *Brain on Fire: My Month of Madness*. London and New York: Simon and Schuster, 2012.

Siri Hustvedt, *The Shaking Woman, or, A History of My Nerves*. New York: Henry Holt, 2010.

Helen Kennerley, *Surviving Stroke: The Story of a Neurologist and His Family*. New York: Robinson, 2020.

Robert McCrum, *My Year Off: Rediscovering Life after a Stroke*. London: Picador, 1998.

Jody Mardula and Frances L. Vaughan, *Mindfulness and*

Stroke: A Personal Journey of Managing Brain Injury. London: Luminate, 2020.

Maria Ross, *Rebooting my Brain: How a Freak Aneurysm Reframed My Life.* Seattle: Red Slice Press, 2012.

May Sarton, *After the Stroke: A Journal.* New York: Norton, 1988.

Lotje Sodderland and Sophie Robinson, *My Beautiful Broken Brain.* [Documentary film.] Netflix Studios, 2014.

Jill Bolte Taylor, *My Stroke of Insight: A Brain Scientist's Personal Journey.* London: Hodder and Stoughton, 2008.

Stephen Trombley, *At a Stroke: Diary of a Recovery.* Independent: 2018.

Brain-related critical writing

Benjamin Bergen, *Louder Than Words: The New Science of How the Mind Makes Meaning* (New York: Basic Books, 2012).

Hood, Bruce. *The Self Illusion: Why There is No 'You' Inside Your Head.* London: Constable, 2012.

Andy Clark, *Supersizing the Mind: Embodiment, Action and Cognitive Extension.* Oxford: Oxford University Press, 2011.

Antonio Damasio, *The Feeling of What Happens.* London: Heinemann, 2000.

— *Self Comes to* Mind. London: Random House, 2010.

Stanlislas Dehaene, *Consciousness and the Brain.* New York: Viking, 2014.

Ilit Ferber, 'A Wound without Pain: Freud on Aphasia', *Naharaim*, Vol. 4, 2010, pp. 133-51.

Sigmund Freud, *On Aphasia.* New York: Literary Licensing, 2011. First published in German in 1891.

Trevor A. Harley, *The Psychology of Language.* London and New York: Psychology Press, 2014.

John Kounios, 'The neuroscience behind epiphanies', 26 June, 2012, See: https://www.youtube.com/watch?v=7uyw5y_tHEM&t=17s [Accessed 29 October 2019].

Joseph LeDoux, *The Emotional Brain.* New York: Weidenfeld and Nicolson, 1998.

Catherine Malabou, *What Should We Do with Our Brain?* New York: Fordham, 2008. Trans. Sebastian Rand. First published in French in 2004.

— *The Ontology of the Accident: An Essay on Destructive Plasticity.* Trans. Carolyn Shread. Cambridge: Polity, 2012. First published in French in 2009.

— *The New Wounded: From Neurosis to Brain Damage.* Trans. Steven Miller. New York: Fordham, 2012. First published in French in 2007.

Daniel Margulies, *Untitled* (2008). See: https://vimeo.com/ 9871689.

Jason Tougaw, 'Brain Memoirs, Neuroscience and the Self', *Literature and Medicine*, Vol. 30. Number 1, Spring 2012, pp.171-92. DOI: 10.1353/lm.2012.0007.

— 'Touching Brains', *Modern Fiction Studies*, Vol. 61. Number 2, Summer 2015, pp. 335-58.